A FUTURE BUILT ON FAITH

So then, as you received Jesus as Lord and Christ, now live your lives in him, be rooted in him and built up on him, held firm by the faith you have been taught, and overflowing with thanksgiving.
(*Colossians 2:6–7*)

To Jane Livesey CJ and Corinne Gibbons who each, in your own way, have taught me what it means to be a sister.

Gemma Simmonds CJ, *Editor*

A Future Built on Faith

RELIGIOUS LIFE AND THE LEGACY OF VATICAN II

the columba press

First published in 2014 by
the columba press
55A Spruce Avenue, Stillorgan Industrial Park,
Blackrock, Co. Dublin

Cover by David Mc Namara
Origination by The Columba Press
Printed by Sprint-Print Ltd, Dublin

ISBN 978 1 78218 099 9

Contents

Acknowledgements

The symposium on religious life which inspired this collection of essays owes a great deal to the continuing commitment and energy of the steering committee of the Religious Life Institute: Benedict Foy (De la Salle Brothers), Anne Griffiths (Ursulines), Damian Howard (Jesuits, Heythrop College), Christopher Jamison (Benedictines), Michael Holman (Jesuits, Heythrop College), Margaret O'Shea (Poor Servants of the Mother of God), Martin Poulsom (Salesians of Don Bosco, Heythrop College), Catherine Skelton (Daughters of St Paul), Kate Stogdon (Cenacle, Heythrop College) and Paul Rout (Franciscans, Heythrop College). A most welcome new addition to the team is Laura Watson, whose calm efficiency as RLI administrator has kept us all on an even keel.

In addition to the RLI steering committee who attended the anniversary symposium our thanks go to the participants whose challenges, reflections and suggestions have been incorporated into the texts. They are: Br Benedict Bedingfield CSJ, Br Mairesean O'Leary CSJ, Br Paul Bednarczyk HC, Sr Ewa Bem IBVM, Dr Richard Finn OP, Sr Maryanne Francalanza FCJ, Sr Margaret Mary Horan CRsS, Sr Cathy Jones RA, Fr Ronnie McAinsh CSsR, Sr Patricia McGee ODC, Abbot Anthony Maggs CRL, Prof. Paul Murray, Dr Susan O'Brien, Ms Catherine Sexton, Dr James Sweeney CP, Sr Bridget Tighe FMDM and Dr Erik Varden OCSO.

The Religious Life Institute once again thanks the Conference of Religious of England and Wales for its financial support. The RLI is one of a number of institutes within Heythrop College and relies for the success of all its activities on the help of the college's administrative and support staff. Particular thanks for their practical and professional support of the symposium are owed to: Nadeem Ahmad, Chris Clark and the catering staff of ABM Catering, Pam Charlton, Judith Crimmins and James Spare.

Thanks also to Corinne Gibbons of Sussex Secretaries for her excellent transcripts of Archbishop Tobin's talks and to Patrick O'Donoghue of Columba Press for his unfailing patience and support in the production and publishing of this book.

Gemma Simmonds CJ,
Director,
Religious Life Institute,
Heythrop College,
University of London

Contributors

MARK BARRETT OSB is a Benedictine monk of Worth Abbey in Sussex, UK. He is Chairman of the English Benedictine Congregation Monastic Theology Commission, and has recently become Co-leader of the Compass Programme (www.compass points.org.uk), a programme of vocational discernment, based at Worth. Mark's doctoral studies addressed issues of spiritual reading in the refounded seventeenth-century English Benedictine Congregation, by focussing on the writings of Fr Augustine Baker OSB. He is presently engaged in a congregation-wide consultation of monasteries, on behalf of the English Benedictine Congregation general chapter intended to lead to a new theological articulation of English Benedictine identity and mission. Mark joined the staff of Heythrop College in 2013.

BENEDICT FOY FSC is a De La Salle Brother and lives in Oxford where he is allegedly retired. He spent forty years teaching in approved schools and in a comprehensive school in Cardiff. He was director of St Cassian's Retreat Centre for young people for five years and had a four-year sabbatical with the Jesuits in Santa Clara University, CA. He was College Chaplain in a multicultural and multifaith school in London for twelve years. Presently he is responsible for formation across the De La Salle network in Great Britain and vocation promotion, and is an original member of the Religious Life Institute Committee.

VIVIENNE KEELY CHF lived in Australia from 1974 to 2011, when she was elected Congregational Leader of the Sisters of the Holy Faith, having served a term on the General Council and two terms as regional leader for Australia/New Zealand. Vivienne was involved in primary, secondary and third level education having held teaching posts in Church History at the Catholic Institute of

Sydney and at St Andrew's Greek Orthodox Theological College. An early medieval historian by training, specialising in the history of sixth-century Gaul, she was director of postgraduate studies at the Sydney College of Divinity for eleven years and most recently was Dean of Studies at the Parramatta Diocesan Seminary. Vivienne served on several diocesan and national bishops' committees for continuing education of the clergy, including the permanent diaconate, and inter-religious dialogue.

PATRICIA RUMSEY PC (Sr Francisca) is Abbess of the Poor Clare Monastery in Arkley and a lecturer in Christian Liturgy at Sarum College. Her most recent publication is *Women of the Church: The Religious Experience of Monastic Women* (Dublin: Columba, 2011). This study articulates her deep concern at the way women religious (and especially monastic women) are still not considered capable of organising their own way of life and the ambivalent attitude of Roman legislation towards women. Her academic interests are: liturgy, especially the early history of the Liturgy of the Hours; early and women's monasticism; Franciscan studies; feminist issues.

GEMMA SIMMONDS CJ is a member of the Congregation of Jesus, teaches Pastoral Theology & Spirituality at Heythrop College, University of London and is Director of the Religious Life Institute. After ten years in teaching she worked as chaplain in the Universities of Cambridge and London and since her return from study and work among women and street children in Brazil in 1992 has been a chaplaincy volunteer in Holloway Prison. Gemma is on the provincial leadership team of her congregation, editor of *A Future Full of Hope?* (Dublin: Columba, 2012) and has been working in national and international religious & priestly formation since the early 1990s. She is a regular broadcaster on the BBC.

BRIAN TERRY SA, a native of Washington, DC, is presently the Novice Director in Assisi of the Friars of the Atonement and an invited professor of Ecumenism at the Angelicum, Rome. He started his ministerial life as a youth minister in McLean, Virginia before entering the order. He has served as a Friar in Pastoral Ministry, Alcohol and Drug Addiction Rehabilitation and Ecumenical Ministry. Fr Brian is interested in studying the 'human in sacrament', an interdisciplinary dialogue of developmental psychology and sacramental theology. He gives workshops on topics related to initial and ongoing formation, ecumenism and sacraments.

JOSEPH TOBIN CSsR has been a Redemptorist missionary since 1973. Ordained a priest in 1978, he spent the first thirteen years of ministry in service to communities of Hispanic immigrants in the central United States and Canada, also serving six years in the government of his province. He served two terms as superior general (1997–2009). He was elected to two terms as the vice president of the Union of Superiors General. In 2010 he was named by Pope Benedict XVI as archbishop secretary of the Congregation for Institutes of Consecrated Life and Societies of Apostolic Life. He was ordained to the episcopacy as archbishop of Indianapolis on 9 October 2012.

ERIK VARDEN OCSO is a native of Norway and currently acting superior of the Cistercian community at Mount Saint Bernard Abbey in Leicestershire. He has spent time teaching at the Pontifical Athenaeum of Sant'Anselmo in Rome. Erik is engaged in research on the early history of Syriac and Byzantine monasticism and is interested in the challenges posed by the transmission of monastic life: how do we pass on a 'charism'? How do we maintain 'tradition' as a living, forward-looking reality?

THOMAS R. WHELAN CSSP is a Spiritan missionary from Ireland, and worked in Sierra Leone for twelve years, a short part of that time in Liberia. Four of these years were spent in parish ministry, and most of the rest working in the Inter-Territorial seminary in Liberia (later Sierra Leone), most of this in the civil wars that engulfed both countries. He holds a primary degree in music, and later studied theology at the Gregorian University in Rome, specialising in liturgical theology (at Sant'Anselmo). Since returning to Ireland in the mid-nineties he has lectured at the Kimmage Mission Institute and is currently Dean of the Faculty of Theology at the Milltown Institute in Dublin, where he lectures in liturgical and sacramental theology. He has a particular interest in issues relating to liturgical theology; textual study of early liturgical sources; liturgical translation; Eucharist; ordained ministry; theology and music; and the relationship between worship and justice.

Introduction

Gemma Simmonds CJ

Since the publication of the Religious Life Institute's first book, *A Future Full of Hope?* in 2012 I have been asked to give a number of talks and interviews based on its content. I have found myself insisting, when the book is mentioned, on the inclusion of the question mark at the end so that its title has become, in verbal form, *A Future Full of Hope Question Mark*. This is not because I have no hope in the future of religious life, but because I am a realist, and can see all too easily, through the work of the Religious Life Institute, the pressures which are weighing on many religious congregations across the world. For hope to be a virtue it precisely requires us to rely on the providence of God rather than on our own strength, whether in numbers, new recruits, renewal programmes, restructuring or any of the things we find necessary to keep alive what the church and many outside its confines still treasure in this way of life.

Encouraged by the success of *A Future Full of Hope?* we decided to venture on into a second collection. Like the first book, this one is based on a series of papers given at a symposium, this time held in Heythrop College, University of London, to celebrate the fiftieth anniversary of the Second Vatican Council and in particular its document on the religious life *Perfectae Caritatis*. The symposium itself was chiefly held in order to welcome Archbishop Joseph Tobin CSsR, then Secretary of the Congregation for Institutes of Consecrated Life and Societies of Apostolic Life, and to hear his 'view from the bridge'. It speaks volumes for his generosity and commitment to the task that he travelled to England for both the symposium and a subsequent greatly appreciated study day attended by over two hundred religious the day after he received news of his appointment as Archbishop of Indianapolis, USA. The opening chapter of the book is taken from his talks at the symposium and the study day. Lack of space has sadly meant the editing out of the vivid and humorous illustrations of his many shrewd points, mostly culled from wide experience both at the Vatican and as general superior of the Redemptorist order.

The chapters of this book are mainly the contribution of their authors, each an authority on religious life in her or his own right. But the papers given on the day of the symposium were redrafted in the light of group discussion and personal contributions made by the remarkable group of religious and scholars who attended it and whose names are listed in the acknowledgements. We consider ourselves immensely privileged to have been able to gather so many wise heads together. Some brought the experience of decades to the table, others the fresh enthusiasm of newer vocations and recent congregations. Between monastic contemplatives, mendicants, canonical, apostolic and missionary congregations, we covered virtually all bases, and the particular theological and practical insights of lay people were another bonus. While wanting to avoid any hint of tokenism, we wanted contributions that looked at the Council and its document on religious life from the particular perspectives of the very different sectors within religious life. What is remarkable is the level of crossover we find, so that issues of identity or of the relationship of religious life to the wider church reappear whether among male monastics or women in simple vows. Other repeated themes, whether in looking at the time of the Council or assessing its impact and interpretation by religious are: a golden-age mentality, whether by those looking back nostalgically at a pre-conciliar age or by those who look at the heady days of the immediate post-Council, the perceived preference in Rome for the emerging ecclesial movements over the less biddable religious orders, and the apparent loss of confidence in religious on the part of the church hierarchy and, on the other hand, the impression given by some religious that their charism-driven mission is completely separate from the mission of God in the church.

14

Archbishop Tobin's chapter offers us an overview of the issues currently facing religious life. Coming from his work at the time in the Vatican curial dicastery for religious life it is painted in broad-brush strokes, not evading critical questions, but manifesting a quiet confidence in the Holy Spirit at work among religious. It also, understandably, emphasises the ecclesial nature of the call to consecrated life while acknowledging that religious life, by its very nature and history, models a different kind of church than that often reflected within the structures of the institution. The original title of his symposium talk was 'The View from the Bridge'. What comes across is not only the global overview one would expect from someone of his administrative background but also the deep wisdom gained through wide experience and a remarkable skill of sympathetic listening to today's religious.

One of the major questions for scholars of *Perfectae Caritatis* is not only its content but its effect on those at whom it was aimed. Part of that therefore concerns its reception history. How did religious receive this document and subsequently implement it? Mark Barrett's scholarly chapter is written from the monastic perspective of the English Benedictine Congregation, but it has implications for all other religious. Who took charge of the adaptations urged by the Council, what authority did they have over the body of their congregation as a whole, and who decided what was or was not an authentic adaptation? He quotes monastic author Robert Barron who writes critically of a 'beige' church that 'went running after modernity, but modernity continued to run away, indifferent to its ardent pursuer'. Barrett, with Erik Varden, is one of the younger contributors to this book and also one of its monastic contributors. There is a similarity to their underlying questions about the effectiveness or otherwise of the post-conciliar renewal and its effect on the identity of religious life.

The question of clericalisation within religious life and, indeed, within the wider church runs as one of many subterranean themes throughout this book. De la Salle brother Benedict Foy raises this question in his contribution about religious life from the perspective of non-clerical male religious brothers. His is also a contrasting voice to that of younger contributors, celebrating the freedom that the Council brought and the return, both in spirit and more recently in structural form, to a more authentic incarnation of the founder's intentions in the spirit of conciliar *ressourcement*.

Vivienne Keely brings her years of leadership and service at diocesan, provincial and general level to bear in her chapter on the question of mission. As one whose office requires her to be part of a discernment process that sends members on mission, she asks searching questions of the impact on religious life of an individualism which is a by-product of secularisation. As a female religious involved in leadership she also challenges the erosion of gains made in the inclusion and appointment of women religious to decision-making roles in mission in the new conservatism that she perceives emerging within the church.

Among women religious, at least, the issue of community has been deeply contentious since the Council. Those apostolic religious who lived in 'total communities', attached to large institutions in which they lived and worked, have especially seen the virtual collapse of the uniformity that formerly marked their life. Patricia Rumsey speaks rather from the perspective of an enclosed contemplative religious of the challenge of community today. She looks at the idealised early Christian community as found in Acts and the effect of that idealisation on the more or less successful subsequent attempts by religious to re-enact community based on those ideals. From the perspective of American sociologists Gerkin and Bellah and also from that of systematic theology in the person of Henri de Lubac, himself one of the great architects of the Council, she explores issues of fragmentation, individualism and community, while also distinguishing between communities and 'lifestyle enclaves'.

Considering the role played by St Francis himself in attempts at dialogue and peacemaking, whether in his native Italy or with the Muslim leader Saladin during the Crusades, it is not surprising to find Franciscan friar Brian Terry exploring religious life as dialogue. In this he is joined in the epilogue by Cistercian Erik Varden. While echoing John Paul II's description of the monk as a 'man of communion', an 'ideal of human fellowship' and a 'bridge of fraternity' he nevertheless explores the tensions that can arise within monastic life when differing understandings of authority and tradition, history and modernity collide.

Thomas R. Whelan has been a missionary and is also a liturgist by academic profession. In 'Religious "Praying Daily" as Church' he looks at the somewhat vexed question of the relationship of religious to the Prayer of the Church and the challenges that face them in their commitment to it in various forms. He offers a theological reflection on the Council's reform of the Liturgy of the Hours, urging religious to look again at what praying as church might mean, especially in light of the paschal mystery and in the specific role of religious to proclaim the *eschaton*. He also offers some suggestions for those struggling with the specific structure and forms of this liturgical prayer, while encouraging a more theological understanding of its importance within the community of believers.

Finally, in an epilogue to the whole collection, Erik Varden speaks for a generation of religious born after the Council, for whom many of its struggles are a matter of history. Through the metaphor of the markedly different approaches to tradition and innovation of Saints Stephen Harding and Bernard of Clairvaux he looks at the need for an intergenerational dialogue that makes of the Council and its reforms neither uncritically reviewed hero nor villain. As such he reminds us that if we are to walk into a future built on faith, it must be with an openness to the questions and challenges of those who come after us, as well as an understanding of those who went before us.

At the time of writing the Episcopal Conference of the Netherlands is reported as predicting that within a decade contemplative/monastic religious life will have ceased to exist in Holland. It is possible that a similar demise of sectors of religious life will have followed in the global north by the time we celebrate the diamond jubilee of the Council. At the same time the Religious Life Institute is undertaking a research project among apostolic women's congregations in the UK and Ireland, funded by the Conrad N. Hilton Foundation, which asks religious what signs of vitality they see within their life. The responses have been remarkably energetic and positive, especially among respondents who were religious before and during the Council. The future is uncertain, but the signs are clear that, in the eyes of those who live it, and of the many who benefit from it in other ways, religious life remains a gift to the church and to the world.

How did we get here?
The Renewal of Religious Life in the Church since Vatican II

Joseph W. Tobin CSsR

Since I recognise that I will be able to treat only a few issues regarding the identity and mission of the consecrated life in the church I hope to develop the theme of recent developments and key concepts in consecrated life against the background of communion and mission, with reference to some concrete issues. I hope also to make some comments regarding the future.

Consecrated life and the church
At the beginning of John Paul II's apostolic exhortation *Vita Consecrata* he writes,

> the consecrated life is at the very heart of the church as a decisive element for her mission, since it manifests the inner nature of the Christian calling and striving of the whole church as the bride towards union with her spouse.[1]

He speaks of it as 'not only ... a help and support for the church' but also

> a precious and necessary gift ... since it is an intimate part of her life, her holiness and her mission. ... A diocese which lacked the consecrated life would not only be deprived of many spiritual

---

[1] John Paul II, Apostolic Exhortation, *Vita Consecrata* (25 March 1996), n. 3 (henceforth *VC*).

gifts, of suitable places for people to seek God, of specific apostolic activities and pastoral approaches, but it would also risk a great weakening of that missionary spirit which is characteristic of the majority of Institutes. There is a duty then to respond to the gift of the consecrated life which the Spirit awakens in the particular churches, by welcoming it with generosity and thanksgiving.[2]

What does it mean to be 'at the heart of the church'? The manifestation of 'the inner nature of the Christian calling' comes from the conciliar decree *Ad Gentes* and what we used to call the foreign missions. Now we realise that the church's very life is missionary. 'The striving of the whole church as the bride' comes from *Lumen Gentium* in the paragraph that begins the treatment on consecrated life. At the Council there was a rather acrimonious debate as to whether religious should be specifically mentioned in the document on the church or not. It was only after the intervention of Paul VI that the decision was made to include what became the sixth chapter of *Lumen Gentium* – the one that deals with religious. A good majority of the bishops were opposed to including a special section on religious life because there was a belief first that religious life was not a fundamental structure of the church but was rather a beautiful decoration that had developed over the course of centuries. They thought that while it beautified the church, it wasn't essential to the church. You could dispense with it and the church would still stand.

Consecrated life is recognised as a gift that enriches both the universal and particular church; this is true, even if, as happens with other vocations in the church, consecrated people may evidence defects and weariness. The text just cited from *Vita Consecrata* reminds us of the ways that consecrated life should enrich the local church by providing:

1. Spiritual gifts.
2. Suitable places for people to seek God.

---

[2] *VC*, 48.

3. 'Specific' apostolic activities and pastoral approaches, that is, pastoral strategies and methods that are not normally found in the institutions of the diocese, especially, its parishes.

Here it is important to note the fact that today the consecrated life in the Western church displays a vast array of expressions, from its most ancient models of male and female monastic life and canons regular, the mendicant orders and the relatively modern forms of apostolic congregations of men or women, to the even more recent expressions of secular institutes and the new so-called 'new forms' of consecrated life. Today the consecrated life witnesses to a revival of classical forms of consecration that appeared in the first centuries of Christianity, such as the *ordo virginum* and hermits. Saint John Paul II recognised with gratitude the diversity of consecrated life, writing,

> How can we not recall with gratitude to the Spirit the many different forms of consecrated life which he has raised up throughout history and which still exist in the Church today? They can be compared to a plant with many branches, which sinks its roots into the Gospel and brings forth abundant fruit in every season of the Church's life. What an extraordinary richness![3]

Consecrated life presents a vast spectrum of expressions. I like to think of it as a tropical rain forest, made up of all sorts of species, some strong and vital, others fragile because of their extreme youth or advanced age. Together, these forms produce an evangelical witness that acts as 'spiritual oxygen', allowing the whole church to breathe. The complexity of consecrated life should caution against facile or superficial judgments, which, today more than ever, risk being unfounded or incomplete.

---

[3] *VC*, 5.

Recent developments in consecrated life

How did we get here? If one wishes to understand better the reality of consecrated life today, it is important to call to mind some of the changes that this particular vocation has experienced in the last four or five decades. The point of departure for a consideration of these changes is certainly the Second Vatican Council. The doctrine of the Council offered two fundamental contributions to consecrated life: a renewed concept of consecrated life and a reminder that it is fundamentally an ecclesial vocation.

As effectively the first doctrinal pronouncement by an ecumenical council on our vocation, *Lumen Gentium* better situates consecrated life in the church, getting beyond the notion of it as a state of perfection. As a matter of fact, all are called to holiness, that is, to perfect charity: this holiness of the church is expressed in many ways in individuals.[4] Consecrated life is one vocation among others, but a vocation with its own specific characteristics. The Council called for

> a greater connection between consecrated life and the Gospel as well as the original charism of each Institute the 'founders' spirit and special aims they set before them as well as their sound traditions ... [and an] adaptation [of religious life] to the changed conditions of our time.[5]

One can see how the Council, after establishing the basis for a new theology of religious life, called for a renewal that would be guided by special attention to two factors: the original charism as well as the present historical moment, but always with the basic aim of living the gospel and following Jesus Christ.

Vatican II provoked a flurry of renewal in most institutes of consecrated life. At the risk of oversimplification, we can say that

---

[4] Second Vatican Council, *Dogmatic Constitution on the Church Lumen Gentium*, 39 (henceforth *LG*).

[5] 'Since the ultimate norm of the religious life is the following of Christ set forth in the Gospels, let this be held by all Institutes as the highest rule.' Second Vatican Council, Decree on the Adaptation and Renewal of Religious Life, *Perfectae Caritatis*, 2 (henceforth *PC*).

the Council and the years that followed brought about some fundamental transitions:

- A passage from the Rule to the Gospel: a realisation that consecrated life is, first and foremost, the *sequela Christi* and the gospel is the essential rule within each and every particular rule.

- A passage from a predominantly juridical-ascetical vision to a more theological understanding of consecrated life.

- A passage from a negative relationship with the world (the result of a fundamental misunderstanding about the notion of *fuga mundi*) to a dialogue with the world and an immersion in it.[6]

- A passage from a spirituality that was nourished principally by a certain devotionalism to a spirituality that is grounded in the Word of God and the liturgy.

- A passage from a religious community that was organised essentially on discipline and observance, to a true gospel fraternity that is characterised by co-responsibility, subsidiarity and more participative forms of government.

There are few ecclesial institutions that have expended such energy, putting into practice the renewal that was mandated by the Council fathers as have the various institutes of consecrated life. This renewal has had also a juridical and institutional dimension. Many special general chapters, having previously revisited the original charism of their respective institutes, strove to reformulate their constitutions and other legislative texts. While this was a profitable exercise, it must also be admitted that one does not change the life of an institute simply by altering its norms and structures.

---

[6] The world is one thing; worldliness is something quite different. The *fuga mundi* cannot become a flight from humanity and history.

Some problematic areas
We should not overlook that fact that, during the period of post-conciliar renewal, consecrated life has profited enormously from the direction of the magisterium, which offered it valuable guidance, beginning with the apostolic exhortation *Evangelica Testificatio* of Paul VI, a text which retains its freshness and utility, to the instruction on 'The Service of Authority and Obedience *Faciem tuam, Domine, requiram*', which was published by our dicastery three years ago.[7] But it is necessary also to point out, even rapidly and in synthetic form, some problematic phenomena that have appeared in consecrated life during the creative and challenging decades that followed the Second Vatican Council.

1. There is a broad anxiety among consecrated people concerning their identity. In an age that is characterised by rapid and fundamental changes in both the church and society, consecrated persons ask, who are we? What really distinguishes our vocation? Where do we 'fit in'?

2. More than in former epochs, the consecrated life has to negotiate its relationship to the local church. Previously, religious men and women tended to think almost exclusively in terms of the church universal. A point about the so-called *fuga mundi* is that if you look at the experience of the monks in the desert, one of the bedrock foundation experiences for our way of life, you could also argue that they were engaged in a *fuga ecclesiae* – a flight from the church. By this I mean what one of my confrères calls 'the institutional church', not the church where we hear the Word of God and celebrate the sacraments of life. There are certainly some values around that lead the Lord today to look at us and say, 'But it can't be that way among you.' We must model a different sort of church.

flight from wld.

---

[7] Paul VI, Apostolic Exhortation, *Evangelica Testificatio* (29 June 1971) and Congregation for Institutes of Consecrated Life and Societies of Apostolic Life, 11 May 2008.

3. The nature and exercise of authority presents another challenging issue. Logically, this issue also touches on the question of obedience. We can see two extremes in consecrated life: one is an attitude that proclaims 'we are all brothers/sisters', but is lived essentially as a sort of anarchy; another is a type of paternalism or maternalism that keeps members in an infantile dependency.

4. The question about charism is essential for the different families of consecrated men and women. There are charisms that retain their unique character and spiritual energy, and are thus capable of inspiring new generations of religious. On the other hand, there are charisms that seem to have been substantially conditioned by particular historical circumstances or connected with a concrete apostolate. The Council echoed the church's constant call for a greater connection between consecrated life and the gospel as well as a connection with the original charism or founding spirit of each institute, and the special aims that the founders set before them as well as their sound traditions, quoting *Perfectae Caritatis*. We can see how the Council, after establishing the basis for a new theology of religious life that is an essential element of the church of communion, called for a renewal that would be guided by special attention to two factors: the original charism as well as the present historical moment, but always with the basic aim of living the gospel and following Jesus Christ. In *A Future Full of Hope?* there is a very good essay on the dangers or pitfalls in returning to the spirit of one's founder or foundress.[8] It shows how sometimes the present problem is that the form of religious life that may have been imposed on a community by the church was not

---

[8] See Mary Finbarr Coffey, 'The Complexities and Difficulties of a Return *ad fontes*', in Gemma Simmonds, ed., *A Future Full of Hope?* (Dublin: Columba Press, 2012), pp. 38–51.

according to the intention of the foundress or founder and so that naturally can lead to creative friction within the body of Christ. If the need for that apostolate disappears, the religious may sense a fundamental rootlessness or *anomie*.

It's been said that the great crisis in apostolic religious life today is that it has to deal with history. The monastic and mendicant orders somehow can have a tradition that allows them to avoid such a violent confrontation. But for those of us who come from an apostolic tradition and are sensitive to the mandate to read signs of times and places, this has produced a lot of uneasiness in us and occasionally friction with different other vocations within the church.

5. The question of mission preoccupies many institutes of consecrated life. There is an effort to overcome a certain dichotomy, insofar as the mission is not something over and above one's consecration; rather, what one does is, in the deepest sense, an essential element of one's special dedication to God. *Vita Consecrata* teaches, 'it can be said that consecrated persons are "in mission" by virtue of their very consecration, to which they bear witness in accordance with the ideal of their Institute.'[9] That same paragraph of the apostolic exhortation affirms: 'It can therefore be said that a sense of mission is essential to every Institute, not only those dedicated to the active apostolic life, but also those dedicated to the contemplative life.' Earlier in the document, John Paul II teaches that 'it can be said that the sense of mission is at the very heart of every form of consecrated life.'[10]

6. In the post-conciliar years there has been great concern for the issue of evangelical poverty: a characteristic of consecrated life that was introduced during the Middle Ages by the mendicant orders. Allied with this issue has been the notion of a preferential option for the poor. The

[9] *VC*, 72.
[10] *VC*, 25.

ideal of institutional poverty has provoked a number of crises among religious families which, at their origin, were established for the poorest of the poor, but now find themselves working among the wealthy.

7. An ever-increasing problem for consecrated life in the West is the decreasing number of religious. In some areas, such as Western Europe, North American and Australia/New Zealand, the crisis has reached dramatic proportions and casts doubt on the future of this vocation in local and national churches. Religious life isn't a problem. Religious life is life, and even more it is a gift that God gives to the church. Religious life as a vocation is an essential element, so the diminishing numbers or ageing of religious has to be a concern of the church. It is an ecclesial question, an ecclesial vocation and therefore an ecclesial worry.

8. At the same time, consecrated life enjoys steady, even explosive growth in the younger churches. This increase carries with it certain challenges, such as that of living communion in a multicultural setting or questions regarding the proper manner of inculturating the charism of an institute.

For consecrated life, the most important ecclesial event after the Second Vatican Council was the IX Ordinary Assembly of the Synod of Bishops that met in 1994 and led to the publication of the apostolic exhortation, *Vita Consecrata* a year and a half later. Limitations of space do not permit me to enter significantly into this crucial document. I simply point out that the exhortation projects a threefold character for consecrated life, which in fact is a reflection of the triple dimension of the church, and, hence, dimensions that necessarily condition consecrated life. These are: 1) the relationship with God or consecration; 2) the fraternal life or communion; and 3) mission. Following a magisterial interest in religious life as discipleship as well as a reflection on its charismatic dimension, the apostolic exhortation of John Paul II emphasised the notion of consecration as the constitutive element of religious life. Consecrated life, then, exists not primarily to do something but to belong to someone.

Some crucial issues for consecrated life today
I would like to say a bit more regarding the crucial issues for
consecrated life as well as some of the challenges it faces. The first
crucial issue concerns the identity of the consecrated man or
woman and his or her relationship to other vocations in the
church. Let us recall an essential element of the doctrine of
Vatican II, already cited here: that all are called to holiness or the
perfection of love. Hence religious life is one manner of living the
baptismal consecration, albeit a vocation that possesses an
'objective excellence'.[11] One of the questions debated during the
Synod of 1994 was whether religious profession represents a new
consecration with respect to the consecration that all receive in
baptism. The apostolic exhortation responded affirmatively:
profession signifies a new and special call and a new and special
gift of the Spirit,

> In the consecrated life, then, it is not only a matter of following
> Christ with one's whole heart, of loving him 'more than father or
> mother, more than son or daughter' (cf. Mt 10:37) – for this is
> required of every disciple – but of living and expressing this by
> conforming one's whole existence to Christ in an all-
> encompassing commitment which foreshadows the eschat-
> ological perfection, to the extent that this is possible in time and
> in accordance with the different charisms.[12]

In a subsequent section, significantly entitled 'New and
Special Consecration', the exhortation teaches,

> In the church's tradition religious profession is considered to be
> *a special and fruitful deepening of the consecration received in Baptism*,
> inasmuch as it is the means by which the close union with Christ
> already begun in Baptism develops in the gift of a fuller, more
> explicit and authentic configuration to him through the pro-
> fession of the evangelical counsels.[13]

There clearly is a need for theologians of consecrated life to
help us better understand the nature of the identity and
specificity of this vocation. It should be kept in mind, however,

---

[11] cf. *VC*, 18.
[12] *VC*, 16.
[13] *VC*, 30.

that, in the past, some concrete elements contributed to a clearer identity of religious men and women, and today these elements are less decisive. Some of these might be the missionary engagement, attention to spirituality, the creation and management of important social projects, even a particular attention to theological research. These fields, once areas that were reserved almost exclusively for religious, are now open also to the laity. What is more, an interest in the original forms of religious life, such as the monasticism of Saint Anthony of the Desert, reveals that this vocation was essentially the Christian life lived in a radical manner but, nevertheless, the Christian life.

The pastors of the church ought to respect this search, which can, at times, present a troubling ambiguity, and take particular care not to identify some religious simply with the clerical state, as often happens in relations with religious priests. It should be added that, related to the search for identity, one senses a growing need for communion between the consecrated life and other vocations in the church. The apostolic exhortation, which followed the Synod on the Laity, affirms,

> In Church-Communion, the states of life by being ordered one to the other are thus bound together among themselves. They all share in a deeply basic meaning: that of being the manner of living out the commonly shared Christian dignity and the universal call to holiness in the perfection of love. They are different yet complementary, in the sense that each of them has a basic and unmistakable character which sets each apart, while at the same time each of them is seen in relation to the other and placed at each other's service.[14]

There is little doubt that a serious responsibility of the local bishop is to favour and promote this complementarity, so that it may become a resource for the diocese instead of a cause for useless competition, for example, between the diocesan and religious clergy.

---

[14] John Paul II, Apostolic Exhortation, *Christifideles Laici*, 55.

Primacy of God

This second issue is directly related to the question of identity. Religious life was born as an affirmation of the absolute claim of God on human beings and, as historians point out, at the time in history when martyrdom ceased to be a feature of Christian communities, leading to a diminishing appreciation for the radical character of the gospel. Thus, an affirmation of the primacy of God, the One who is to be loved with an undivided heart, represents the first and most essential quality of the consecrated life. God is the One who gives reason to and motivation for the conduct of consecrated men and women. There is a danger that, because of their dedication to pastoral activity or works of service, consecrated persons inordinately sacrifice their witness to a radically Christian life, that is, to the effort towards being, first and foremost, seekers of God and true Christians. Without such an effort, there cannot be a true consecrated life. Without this dimension that touches on the being of consecrated people, all their activity can lose its fundamental *raison d'être*.

Gospel-based fraternity

I would like to emphasise this third challenge, even if this issue usually is not evident to those who are not members of the consecrated life. In reality, fraternal life that is lived in community demands a great deal of spiritual energy as well as time and space that are dedicated intelligently and with a loving spirit. The rediscovery of the fraternal life as a sort of *schola amoris*, based on a common following of Christ and interlaced each day by a rigorous self-discipline, has been one of the great achievements of recent years. The way religious live together, which has been an essential element from the very beginning of consecrated life, is itself a gift of the Spirit and a way of radically fulfilling the commandment of love. A beautiful instruction from our dicastery, *Fraternal Life in Community*, offers a number of valuable suggestions for carrying out this commitment.[15] Fraternity needs

---

[15] CIVCSVA, *Fraternal Life in Community* (2 February 1994).

to be continuously rediscovered as the vital space, the indispensable 'habitat' for this vocation as well as the point of departure for its mission and the place to which it constantly returns. The leadership of the institute should care for this essential dimension of the life of consecrated persons, even if this means that they might decline a particular pastoral service to the local church. Here it is helpful to recall a portion of the instruction *Fraternal Life in Community*,

> All must be reminded that fraternal communion, as such, is already an apostolate; in other words, it contributes directly to the work of evangelization. The sign *par excellence* left us by Our Lord is that of lived fraternity.... For this reason, 'the effectiveness of religious life depends on the quality of the fraternal life in common'.[16]

In summary, these three issues: identity, the primacy of God and fraternal life in community, are challenges for consecrated life. To these we might also add mission. I believe, however, that the issue of mission is widely acknowledged, especially among congregations of men or women religious that are dedicated to apostolic or diaconal service. As the magisterium on consecrated life has affirmed, a clear emphasis on the primacy of God, making it an effective priority rather than merely theoretical, together with a truly fraternal life that is lived in the spirit of the gospel, is already a 'mission' for religious men and women.

SOME CONCRETE QUESTIONS

Consecrated life and the particular church
In the wake of the Second Vatican Council, both the theology of the particular church as well as that of consecrated life have developed significantly. However, such development has not been accompanied by a successful integration of the two. Here I would simply note two matters which call for further reflection, even experimentation. On the one hand, consecrated life needs

---

[16] Ibid, 54.

to be inserted adequately within the particular church, since it is within a local church that it lives and where the universal church is made present.[17] On the other hand, it should not be forgotten that consecrated life is called to witness to the universal church within the reality of a particular church. *Vita consecrata* clearly affirms this mission:

> All this brings out the character of universality and communion proper to Institutes of Consecrated Life and to Societies of Apostolic Life. Because of their supra-diocesan character, grounded in their special relation to the Petrine ministry, they are also at the service of cooperation between the particular churches, since they can effectively promote an 'exchange of gifts' among them, and thus contribute to an inculturation of the Gospel which purifies, strengthens and ennobles the treasures found in the cultures of all peoples.[18]

In effect, different particular churches, especially in Asia and Africa, have directly experienced the contribution of religious men and women, who came from other dioceses and were present at the birth and growing years of these young churches. Frequently religious bring to their diocese of origin the requests for help to these young churches and thus can favour a real 'exchange of gifts'. Hence, the church should avoid, if I might use a neologism, an excessive *diocesisation* of consecrated life; that is, acting as if a religious institute, which is international by nature, instead is perceived only in the function of a particular church. It is interesting to note that *Propositio 29* of the Synod of Bishops on Consecrated Life recommended that religious give greater attention to the particular church and that bishops value and welcome the charism of consecrated life, making room for religious within the pastoral plan of the diocese. What does this mean, in practical terms?

First, there is a need for mutual respect and effective communication between the diocesan bishop and the major superiors of religious who serve in the diocese. Reciprocal visits have also proven to be helpful in fostering communion between

---

[17] *Lumen Gentium*, 23.
[18] *VC*, 47.

the diocesan bishop and religious. The bishop ought to appreciate persons and structures that will enhance his pastoral care for religious, such as the diocesan vicar or delegate for consecrated life. The bishop may wish to include religious in some of the diocesan offices or organisms, such as presbyteral or pastoral councils. Special attention should be given to the inclusion of women religious, who make up nearly eighty per cent of the consecrated life. Speaking about the relationship between the bishop and women religious, the *Directory for the Pastoral Ministry of Bishops* recommends,

> The Bishop should also be vigilant that consecrated women are given sufficient opportunities for participation in different diocesan structures, such as diocesan and parish pastoral councils, where these exist, in the various diocesan commissions and delegations, and in the direction of apostolic and educational initiatives in the diocese. They should also be involved in the decision-making processes, especially in matters directly affecting them. In this way they can bring to the service of God's people their particular sensitivities and their missionary fervour, their unique gifts and the fruits of their experience (cf. *Vita Consecrata*, 104).[19]

The autonomy of religious

Canon 586, §1 of the CJC recognises a 'just autonomy of life, especially of governance' for institutes of consecrated life; Canon 732 makes a similar recognition in the case of societies of apostolic life. This autonomy is the means by which a single institute of consecrated life or society of apostolic life can enjoy in the church its own internal discipline and preserve intact its own charism and identity. It is in this sense that one should read the word 'patrimony' in the final phrase of Canon 586, §1: and can preserve whole and entire the patrimony described in Canon 578, since the word 'charism' is not used in the Code.

---

[19] Congregation for Bishops, *Directory for the Pastoral Ministry of Bishops* (Vatican City: Libreria Editrice Vaticana, 2004), n. 104.

With regard to their proper bishop, a 'just autonomy' is attributed also to institutes and societies of diocesan right by Canon 594, which judges as illegitimate any interference by the bishop in the internal life of the institute. The local ordinary is charged with safeguarding and protecting the just autonomy of institutes of either pontifical or diocesan right that are present in the diocese. Hence, the bishop is never considered as the superior of an institute. Even in the case of institutes of diocesan right, the Code never applies to the bishop any title that is proper of a religious superior, such as 'Moderator'. The preferred phrase is typically something like (the institute) 'remains under the special care of the diocesan bishop'.

The just autonomy of institutes of consecrated life and societies of apostolic life should not be understood simply as respect for their freedom but rather as a requirement of the church herself, for whom the variety of charisms in the individual institutes represents a rich source of evangelical witness and pastoral activity.

In Canon 586, §1, the formulation indicates that a just autonomy is not the fruit of a concession by canon law, but rather a natural right of each institute which the legislator recognises by the act of giving juridical approval to institutes of consecrated life and societies of apostolic life.

Obviously, the just autonomy we are speaking about does not signify in any way a total independence from legitimate authority; for example, that of the Pope, as well as that of the diocesan bishop.

Vocations from one country that help others
I would simply like to touch on this matter, which may concern some dioceses. If in the past many men and women religious served as missionaries in Asian or African countries, today it is increasingly common, especially in Europe and North America, that religious institutes with declining numbers and an advanced average age, seek the help of young Asian or African religious in order to sustain their foundations. Such cooperation may well be the result of intelligent and careful planning that brings about a

valid 'exchange of gifts' among different nations and cultures. However, at times this cooperation happens without sufficient attention to potential problems that are inherent to multicultural living and ministry and, consequently there is little preparation of the religious themselves. There is the risk of a sort of trafficking of women (or men) religious and the results can be scandalously antithetical to the ideals of consecrated life. Such problems are particularly troublesome when we speak of cloistered monasteries of contemplative nuns.

Mission

I think for most of our institutes the question of mission preoccupies us. There is an effort to overcome a certain dichotomy insofar as mission is not something that we do outside the house, but then we become something else when we come home. Our lives and the lives of our institutes is mission and some institutes say in their constitutions, 'Our community life is the first proclamation of the gospel.' So the way we live together announces who we are as disciples of Jesus. It can be said that consecrated people are on mission by virtue of their very consecration, to which they bear witness in accordance with the ideal of their institute. *Vita Consecrata* affirms, 'It can therefore be said that a sense of mission is essential to every institute, not only those dedicated to the apostolic life, but also those dedicated to the contemplative life.'[20] That should not be surprising when we realise that the woman who is patroness of overseas missions, was herself a contemplative sister.

Poverty

In the post-conciliar years there has been a great concern for the issue of evangelical poverty, a characteristic of consecrated life that was introduced really during the middle ages by the mendicant orders. Allied with this issue has been the notion of a

---

[20] *Vita Consecrata*, 72.

preferential option for the poor. The ideal of institutional poverty has provoked a number of crises among religious families which at their origin were established for the poorest of the poor but now find themselves working essentially for the wealthy.

Obedience

Most of us have moved in our institutes from a sort of verticalism and dictatorial power of superiors. The passage from a religious community organised essentially on discipline and observance to a gospel fraternity is a change that I think most of us have gone through. But can we be critical about our way of government and leadership today? There's an excellent essay by George Wilson SJ called 'Incumbency or Leadership' and he uses an example there of a criticism he makes of the notion of a servant-leader.[21] He says in his analysis of consecrated life that servant-leadership can lead one to conclude that the principal function of leaders is to meet the needs of the others. Now that sounds quite consonant with the gospel. We wash each others' feet but this is especially true of the one who is called to leadership. But this might absolve the leaders of something much more serious and difficult. The example Wilson uses in his essay is that of a province as a sort of collective of a hundred persons or so riding in a raft down a river with the leadership as the crew. They are going around on the raft questioning everyone to make sure that their needs are being met, and meanwhile nobody notices that the raft is about to go over Victoria Falls.

In the magisterium on superiors it is interesting to see that the superior is the first person to discern the will of God, not the only one, but the one whose responsibility is to ask: what does God require of us today? And then to verify that with her sisters or her brothers.

---

[21] See George B. Wilson, 'Leadership or Incumbency?'
<http://gbwilson.homestead.com/Leadership_or_incumbency.htm>

Eschatological dimension

There is a dimension of religious life that was particularly accentuated in the vision of Vatican II and that perhaps has been forgotten by us and leads us to judge the present moment and our future with a sort of spiritual myopia. I call it the 'forgotten paragraph' and it comes from *Lumen Gentium* and says,

> The people of God have no lasting city here below but look forward to the one that is to come. Since this is so, the religious state ... not only witnesses to the fact of a new and eternal life acquired by the redemption of Christ, but it foretells the future resurrection and the glory of the heavenly kingdom. ... The religious state clearly manifests that the kingdom of God and its needs in a very special way are raised above all earthly considerations. Finally, it clearly shows all people both the unsurpassed breadth of the strength of Christ the King and the infinite power of the Holy Spirit marvellously working in the Church.[22]

This paragraph reminds us of the *eschaton*. It teaches us about the provisory character of every human institution; things pass, but God is eternal. It invites us to think about the significance and destiny of our life. This makes me think that the most important element of religious life is not captured by statistics. I am quick to say that vocation promotion is an essential part of religious life. But to judge religious simply by headcount is a mistake. It is a graver mistake to simply conclude that the diminution of religious is a direct result of the infidelity of religious. I find that to be a silly statement, knowing a bit about religious and how they live their lives today. I think that we ought to be secure enough in our vocation to look at statistics and ask how they are speaking to us.

The testimony, the sign value of our lives says something, and that might be in relationship to statistics. If our life is unidentifiable, if there is nothing that characterises us, then it makes it much more difficult for the sign to be read and to have

---

[22] *Lumen Gentium*, 44.

the other values of our life presented and understood.[23] So the first question that comes out of my reflection on the eschatological dimension of religious life has to do with sign, or the visibility of religious life. It leads us to listen to the Sermon on the Mount and the opening salvo of Jesus Christ after the Beatitudes with a particular sensitivity when he says, 'you are salt for the earth'. We are also light for the world, and light is something that is recognised or at least its absence is felt. So how are we recognised as light and salt? I am not able to reduce that to an article of clothing, but I am asking the more difficult question. If it is not the clothing we wear, what tells people about who we are and associates us with the community that holds certain values?

Celibacy

The crisis of celibacy today is an eschatological crisis. The unclear value that we offer as celibate, consecrated, chaste people can contribute to the disappearing of this possible Christian vocation in the church and in the world. Together with Charles Taylor, I think that, on the one hand, Luther and Calvin were right to condemn the ideology of a spiritual superiority, a sort of caste which infected late medieval monasticism, but they ended up discrediting celibate vocations as such. They began by criticising an exaggeration and finished by eliminating celibacy as a possibility for Christians and thus greatly reduced the range of Christian lives. Today's secular world is another Reformation, not unrelated to the reforming tendencies within the church, where renunciation is not only viewed with suspicion but celibacy is pushed off the radar screen altogether. It's seen as a form of madness or self-mutilation, and what is the result of this? We end up with a much narrower possibility for human beings to live humanly and to live their vocation. This makes it much more possible for people to be lost in a world where hedonism is the operating value. This crisis of eschatology results in the

---

[23] cf. Gemma Simmonds, 'Religious Life: A Question of Visibility', in Gemma Simmonds, ed., *A Future Full of Hope?* (Dublin: Columba Press, 2012), pp. 116–28.

exaggerated homogenisation of life, to make level the playing fields to the point where everybody is expected to live the same way. So proposed originally as an alternative to self-mutilation, it mutilates, it limits and distorts. The true meaning of our consecrated chastity is found in our eschatological vision. The way we look at the future, what we are expecting the future to bring, determines the way we live in the moment and will help us understand whether or not we have oil in the lamp.

Hospitality

A value that is actually more than simple charity but has an eschatological significance that I think is present among religious and has always been present is the value of hospitality. Hospitality in welcoming the stranger is a constant openness on the part of a community that means their own circumscribed reality does not have the final word. They permit the stranger, the other, to come in and be welcome and thereby change that community. I think that those of us who belong to international institutes have an opportunity within many of our own communities, before we talk about migrant ministry or justice for refugees, of welcoming the other because of the international character of our communities. I have seen some very dramatic examples of this in my service to the church. In Siberia I stayed oftentimes with the Friars Minor because they have some well-established communities there. From the very beginning of their service in Siberia, they had made a deliberate decision that they would carry out their mission in international communities. Before they went to Siberia they went to Assisi and lived there for about six months talking about what it was going to be like to live the charism of their order. They saw this as fraternity lived in minority, as strangers in a land where Catholic Christianity, under the Russian legal system, is considered not to be a religion but a cult, in the same category as Jehovah's Witnesses and Scientology. They especially wanted to think about how they would deal with the conflict that would arise among themselves. That sort of preparation gave them the opportunity to prepare to welcome each other in the community and then to be able, as an international community, to welcome the people who would come to them. This is a witness that only religious can offer in a particular way according to *Vita Consecrata*. It says that

> the international institutes can offer an example of fraternity that is more than ever needed in a world that is characterized by exaggerated nationalism even xenophobia.[24]

Why we welcome each other and then, as a community, we welcome the other is because in doing so we are welcoming Christ and we are anticipating his return. I think that among all the images we can use for religious life in the church there is one that comes from what I understand to be the self-understanding of Jesus when He celebrated Passover. There is a marvellous study published in the Biblicum years ago called *Les Quatre Nuits*, which asked what Jesus thought he was doing with his disciples when they celebrated Passover.[25] The study argued that they were celebrating four nights. The central night was the night of the Exodus when the most defining action of God for the people of Israel was that he heard their cries and led them to freedom. The other nights were seen in the light of that night.

The first night is the night of creation when God redeems the world from chaos. The second night is the redemption of Isaac when God intervened to save Isaac and then the Targum, the parable of text that was read in the synagogue and that portion of the book of Genesis, adds that Isaac was thirty-three years old, interestingly enough in the Christian tradition. But we are the fourth night. We certainly share and reflect the liberating power, the creating power of God, but the fourth night had not yet happened when Jesus broke bread with his disciples in the Seder. The fourth night was the return of the Messiah and in many Jewish communities the doors of the synagogue were flung open just in case the Messiah was there. I think our living in the

---

[24] *Vita Consecrata*, 51.
[25] Roger le Déaut, *La Nuit Pascale: Essai sur la signification de la Pâque juive à partir du Targum d'Exode XII* (Pontificium Institutum Biblicum, 42, 1963), p. 423 ff.

function of the One who is to come leads us to a sort of openness to welcome the Messiah as he comes today in view of the time when he will come and restore all things to God. So hospitality, as a classic characteristic of community life, is a characteristic of religious life today. And it means that it is a welcome given to the One who is coming, Jesus our Redeemer, the One who will restore all things to God.

Ars moriendi, ars vivendi

How do we live this in diminished numbers and ageing communities? The first thing is that we don't deny the difficulties, we don't play with the statistics to the point that we can whistle through this crisis. *Vita Consecrata* says,

> the various difficulties stemming from the decline in personnel and apostolates must in no way lead to a loss of confidence in the evangelical vitality of consecrated life which will always be present and active in the Church. New situations and difficulties are therefore to be faced with the serenity of those who know what is required of each individual is not success, but a commitment to faithfulness. What must be avoided at all costs is the actual breakdown of consecrated life, a collapse which is not measured by a decrease in numbers, but by a failure to cling steadfastly to the Lord and to one's personal vocation and mission'[26]

We can see it is not a numbers game in the final order. Our first priority should not be the *ars moriendi* even though we recognise that death is an experience that we all will share. It is the *ars vivendi*, in view of the One who is coming, that we accept, no matter how strong or how vital we are, that that's passing, that God is ultimately faithful to us and that we are faithful to each other so that we can welcome each other. We can welcome new generations and new forms of consecrated life and not marginalise them because they seem to be different from us. We welcome them as a sign that God hasn't given up on us, but he is

---

[26] *Vita Consecrata*, 63.

raising new forms. We can welcome the generational differences in our communities.

I remember having an interesting conversation with Timothy Radcliffe, then Master General of the Order of Preachers, at the time that we were first together at a synod of bishops. I asked how the order was doing in France. Timothy said, 'Rather well. We have forty professed students and the average age of our province in Toulouse is about forty-seven.' Being a good American, I wanted to know in ten easy steps how they had resolved the vocation crisis. Timothy replied, 'I think the first thing you have to say is that a vocation can't be reduced simply to strategies. A vocation is a mystery of love and you have to respect that. However, we, as Dominicans, have made certain decisions on what it means to be a Dominican in France today. And we've changed accordingly. Secondly, I, as Master of the Order, have to get between these young people and the generation of 1968, because if I don't, the friars of '68 will eat those young ones alive.' Several years later I asked the confrères of one of our provinces how the vocation promotion was going. Several said, 'the only ones who are interested are these right-wing nuts.' I replied, 'Why don't you say they are different before you put a more specific label on? At least say they are different from you. Maybe they are asking the same privilege that you asked for, and that's to be different from your elders. And maybe you want to listen to them and see if the charism that God has given to the church through our institute is reflected in their lives or not. I think you would be surprised to find how often it is.'[27]

So the welcoming as a charismatic, eschatological value begins in our communities with those who are different, especially those who are different culturally, because otherwise the first card that is played in a dispute is the cultural card: you don't like me because I am from Lower Slobbovia. Or it's the generational card: how dare you, you've only been a religious for two years and you're questioning me? And it's not simply something that is bad

---

[27] For a continued discussion of this point see the Epilogue to this book, written by Erik Varden OCSO.

behaviour or impolite, it is a short-sightedness that wants to canonise our experience as normative for everybody else rather than seeing how a different opinion, a different experience of living religious life can enrich the way we live in experience.

We also are able to embody in our communities one of the chief prophetic images of the end times: the banquet to which all people will be invited and will enjoy rich and wonderful foods and choice wines. Isaiah must have been a religious to use those examples. The Messianic banquet is modelled by communities where everyone isn't the same but they share the rich food of the Word of God and the heady wine of the charism that has been given to our communities. So the final word of an eschatological character to our lives is the life of hope. Whatever happens to our own institutes, as long as we are living faithfully, really doesn't matter because God is faithful. My prayer for you that are living this horrific and purifying experience of diminishment and age is that you can find the heart, if you don't have it already, to know that even if your strength has been reduced, your productive service, if you want to use raw pragmatic terms, is lessened, you are still living your mission in hope because you know the mission doesn't die with you and you know that you can still offer something. I hope that all of us can live as signs of value that here admit no permanent city but allow us the freedom of living in hope.

Reflection Questions

1. How have you experienced religious life as an ecclesial vocation? What does it mean that religious life 'is at the very heart of the church as a decisive element for her mission'?

2. What do you understand by the five 'passages' that Tobin describes? What difference do you see these shifts as having made to religious life?

3. How do you understand what is said here about the value of hospitality and welcoming as an eschatological sign? What difference might this value make to community life as you currently experience it?

Consider Your Call: A Theology of Monastic Life Today (1978): *A Post-Conciliar Process of Reflection on Monastic Identity*

Mark Barrett OSB

Introduction

It is sometimes said that in traditional monastic congregations we have, so to speak, 'lost our bite'. By this it is suggested that 'monastic life is going through a period not of decadence but of inner poverty ... and cannot for the moment challenge the Church and the world as we ought.'[1] The image of 'loss of bite' to express something amiss in monastic life is both painful and apposite. It conveys the sense that monks and nuns who genuinely believe themselves to be aiming at lives of monastic fidelity are nevertheless proving unequal to the task of presenting the present moment with the full sharpness and vitality of the living gospel. In many contexts, we may appear to be capable only of offering a 'lite' version of monasticism's core demands – effectively a 'beige monasticism', paralleling Fr Robert Barron's better-known bugbear, 'beige Catholicism', which he characterises as 'bland, accommodating, hyper-apologetic, unsure of itself'.[2]

Widespread difficulties in recruitment are only one manifestation of this beigeing of the Benedictines, the blunting of

---

[1] Josephine Mary Miller, 'Bringing New Life to the Communities' (unpublished paper, July 2005).

[2] Robert Barron, 'The Depressing Pew Forum Study', *Word on Fire* [website], October 2010 <http://www.wordonfire.org/Written-Word/articles-commentaries/October-2010/The-Depressing-Pew-Forum-Study.aspx>

monastic bite, but they do serve to highlight it. One American abbot writes,

> instead of seeing that I am an instrument to convert and call, or that I am part of a community which is such an instrument, what I seem to see instead, at least in North America and Europe, is religious communities which are almost without vocations, aging, becoming increasingly precarious, and an ongoing onslaught against Christianity, and its fading from the mind and heart of the West.[3]

At the same time, we note that the rising generation of young women and men in the West, who are 'growing up in a world of relativism, political correctness, and ambivalence' are, perhaps as a consequence, 'looking for a defined identity as Catholic Christians', and for vital and visible ecclesial modes of enacting that identity.[4] It might therefore be argued that a significant aspect of the 'loss of bite' of traditional monastic congregations is to be located in our having, for the most part, failed to connect with this rising generation, at least in terms of presenting them with the monastic vocation as just such a vital and visible mode of Catholic living.

It is not my intention here to indulge in yet another jeremiad on the future of monastic life, lamenting the declining numbers of monks and nuns. Rather, I find it potentially significant that the pursuit of a 'defined identity' is, in some sense, the common preoccupation both of the young and of Benedictine monastics. However, there is a notable difference (at least in broad-brush terms) between the approach taken by each of these groups to the topic of identity. Whereas for the young the issue of religious identity, although manifesting a challenging series of demands in terms of lifestyle choices, appears to function as a relatively

---

[3] Thomas Frerking, 'Restoring the EBC's "Bite"' (unpublished paper, November 2006).

[4] Paul Bednarczyk, 'Implications of the NRVC/CARA Study on the Future of Religious Vocations', The J.S. Paluch Vocation Seminar Address, *The Roman Catholic Diocese of Brooklyn* [website], 18 August 2009 <http://dioceseofbrooklyn.org/wpcontent/uploads/2012/05/NRVC_CARA-Study_Future-Implications.pdf>

straightforward positive value, for some traditional monastic congregations the issue of a 'defined [monastic] identity', while notionally affirmed as a value, has been in practice contentious and continues to be controverted. Might it be that this disjunction is a factor contributing to the loss of monastic 'bite'?

The American-Cassinese Benedictine Congregation preserves on its website a detailed, thoughtful 'Statement on the American-Cassinese Benedictine Monastic Life', entitled *Renew and Create*, the work of its general chapter of 1969. *Renew and Create* quite unambiguously states the view that 'the most basic problem in our Congregation today is that of Benedictine identity'. Unless the presence of this statement on the congregational website is of historical interest only (and this does not appear to be the case), this sentence may be taken at face value as having a continuing contemporary application. *Renew and Create* elaborates the 'problem … of Benedictine identity' in this way:

> on the institutional level the root Benedictine problem facing our communities is this: a lack of clarity concerning the basic orientation of Benedictine life as a distinct form of Christian life having a specific function in the Church; a consequent lack of clarity and inner coherence between elements of spiritual doctrine and the concrete structures of living which *de facto* shape the life of our communities; and a resultant confusion concerning the concrete manner in which our monasteries ought to effect creative adaptation to contemporary realities. This root problem is clearly manifested in specific elements of spiritual doctrine and institutional structure.[5]

This is an astute and incisive analysis; it is elaborated in further detail within the document, but this introductory account itself repays some unpacking.

Renew and Create states the 'root problem' as a lack of 'clarity concerning the basic orientation of Benedictine life'. Such clarity is a fundamental issue in the theology of the monastic life, having to do with an appropriate understanding of monasticism as 'a

---

[5] American-Cassinese Congregation, 'Renew and Create: A Statement on the American-Cassinese Benedictine Monastic Life, Thirty-Sixth General Chapter, June 1969', *American-Cassinese Congregation* [website], 22 April 2009. <http://www.osb.org/amcass/renew/> Part 1 & 2.

distinct form of Christian life' with its own inner integrity, and with the articulation of the place and function of that integral form of life within the church. Absent such an articulation of a 'defined identity' on the part of monastics, the American-Cassinese statement argues, 'inner coherence' between the lived spirituality of monastics and the 'concrete structures of living' to be found in their monasteries becomes well-nigh impossible to achieve. In practical terms, we might suggest, this could well result in a situation where individual monks and nuns find themselves obliged to discover and live out individualised spiritual paths which have no necessary relationship with (and might, in the worst case scenario, be actively at odds with) the patterns of living, working and praying which are practised in their monasteries. The passage from *Renew and Create* goes on to make the point that once this is happening, both institutional structures and spiritual doctrines in monastic houses may begin to display 'adaptation to contemporary realities' which reflect the confusions consequent upon the lack of inner coherence between spirituality and structure at the basic level of monastic identity.

With the authors of *Renew and Create*, I appreciate that it would be mistaken to 'understand identity in some static way as if the problem could be solved by the discovery and establishment of some timeless definition of the monastic life'. Nevertheless, I share the Cistercian Michael Casey's view that 'a monk is constituted as such by living within an *evident tradition*. Genuine monasticism is not self-generating. It cannot be the product of individual self-expression because the goal of monastic living is self-transcendence.'[6] (Italics added) The question of defining monastic identity, as the American Cassinese document makes very clear, has not gone away.

Against this background, the scope of the present chapter is modest. I shall not here attempt directly to address issues of how we should define and articulate monastic identity. Nevertheless, it is timely, as we reflect upon the reception of Vatican II, to

---

[6] Michael Casey, 'Thoughts on monasticism's possible futures', in Patrick Hart, ed., *A Monastic Vision for the 21st Century: Where Do We Go from Here?* (Cistercian Publications, 2006), p. 24–5.

examine one post-conciliar attempt to do just this: that of the English Benedictine Congregation (EBC). My aim will be to discover whether this process from forty years ago offers any lessons to the present moment. To that end, I shall explore some aspects of the process which led to the writing and publication of the book *Consider Your Call: A Theology of Monastic Life Today* in 1978.[7] This text has been understood within the EBC as 'the book that represents the EBC's post-conciliar rethought Statement on Monasticism'.[8] I shall suggest that there are some aspects of the process then employed, and of the book's self-presentation as a work of theological reflection upon monastic identity, which have contributed to that volume's rapid dating, and to its seeming neglect as a working tool for contemporary English Benedictines. Perhaps what I believe must ultimately be judged the failure of *Consider Your Call* is a factor contributing to the 'loss of bite' presently being experienced by the houses of the EBC?

Consider Your Call: A Theology of Monastic Life Today (1978)
Two rather different books emerged from the EBC in the process of renewal that followed Vatican II. The first, and the weightiest, of these was *Consider Your Call: A Theology of Monastic Life Today*, a volume of some four hundred and fifty pages of theological reflection on Benedictine monastic identity. Commissioned by the general chapter of the EBC and published in 1978, the book was the outcome of about eight years of work, by a significant range of EBC monks and nuns. At first glance, *Consider Your Call* appears to enjoy some form of quasi-official status as an EBC statement of Benedictine monastic identity. It was followed in 1982 by a second book, *A Touch of God*, a much shorter and self-consciously popularised presentation of EBC spirituality intended for a lay audience, structured around a series of autobiographical essays by its eight EBC contributors. Here, I shall for the most part be concerned with the process that created

---

[7] Daniel Rees et al., *Consider Your Call: A Theology of Monastic Life Today* (London, SPCK, 1978).

[8] *The Ampleforth Journal*, Autumn 1978, p. 22.

Consider Your Call, but I shall also refer briefly to *A Touch of God* below.

In the preface to *Consider Your Call* the Chairman of the Commission that produced the book, Fr Daniel Rees OSB, sets out the immediate background against which the eight-year process leading to its publication should be situated, namely 'the mandate to renew themselves which the Second Vatican Council issued to all religious congregations in the decree *Perfectae Caritatis*'.[9] Between Vatican II and the beginning of EBC's theological responses to the Council stands one other specifically Benedictine event of some significance here and this too is noted in the preface. In the immediate aftermath of the Council, the 1967 Congress of Abbots (a meeting in Rome of all the abbots of the Benedictine Confederation) created and officially adopted its own renewed statement of monastic identity, entitled 'A Statement on Benedictine Life' (SoBL).

The complex factors involved in creating and promulgating a document on monastic identity across a body as diverse as the Benedictine Confederation are apparent from the outset of the document. At one level, SoBL wishes to be understood as authoritatively setting forth the 'essential criteria of the Benedictine way of life'.[10] The introduction to SoBL states, 'a certain way of life, namely the one established by the Rule [of St Benedict], should be genuinely characteristic of all Benedictine monks', going on to affirm that 'it is only by conformity to these principles – basic to the whole Benedictine way of life – that any community could be, and call itself, a Benedictine community'.[11] But only a few sentences later these same basic principles by which an individual monk is to live, and a monastery is to be judged as a Benedictine community, elide seamlessly into mere

---

[9] Rees, *Consider Your Call*, p. xiii.
[10] 'A Statement on Benedictine Life', Adopted by the Congress of Abbots held in Rome in September 1967 and translated into English by monks and nuns of the EBC, (Ware: Carmelite Monastery, 1968), p. ii (henceforth SoBL).
[11] SoBL, p. 8.

talking points around issues of unity and plurality, which might 'assist post-conciliar renewal'.[12]

Behind this seeming volte-face lurks one of the great imponderables of Benedictine life. The Confederation (of which the Congress of Abbots is a manifestation) is a worldwide union of Benedictine congregations, each of which retains its own autonomy, while these constituent congregations are themselves more or less loose affiliations of autonomous monastic houses. Thus, while all the world's abbots are fully entitled to gather in Congress and teach in the name of the Confederation, very few of the world's monasteries are under any specific obligation to listen to what they say, let alone act upon it. Perhaps one might describe the Congress itself as somewhat short on 'bite'.

Glossing this ambiguous perspective, the foreword to the English-language edition of SoBL (written by three EBC abbots) comments that the Congress document

> is not meant to be a 'blue-print' for the future of monasticism, nor is its intention to give definitive answers to the different questions that might be asked in connection with monastic life, its doctrine and practice, in our day. Its aim is more limited … this statement on monastic life is to provide monks and nuns with a starting point for their own reflections on the doctrinal basis and practice of the Benedictine life.

SoBL was privately published by the EBC in English in the UK in 1968, and in 1969 'provisional constitutions [for the EBC] were drafted where the legal provisions were intercalated by expositions of spirituality extracted from SoBL' in response to *Ecclesiae Sanctae*. Rees notes that the post-conciliar *motu proprio* contained

> a very emphatic injunction that the renewed constitutions should not be purely juridical in character but should also express the evangelical and theological principles concerning religious life and its incorporation in the Church, and 'an apt and accurate formulation in which the spirit and aims of the founder should be clearly recognised and faithfully preserved.

---

[12] SoBL, p. 11.

This 'apt and accurate formulation' of monastic identity might have been found by the EBC in SoBL, but, Rees informs us,

> since the Congress [of Abbots] is a federation of representatives of many different species of Benedictine life, its Statement was inevitably very general in character and could not be taken as an adequate expression of the differing traditions and interpretations of monastic theology to be found among its members.

Rees' rhetoric here transforms almost into an impersonal law of nature ('was inevitably', 'could not be taken') what was in fact a specific decision by the authorities of the EBC effectively to reject SoBL as the substantial basis for renewing its own monastic life, and instead to work independently (autonomously?) on its own congregational statement. Viewed more positively, one might say that the EBC opted to follow the injunction of SoBL that the Congress of Abbots' document be seen as a basis for 'discovering as accurately as possible the exact goal of their renewal' by individual monastic congregations, and undertake a more local project; nevertheless, to a contemporary reader Rees' somewhat dismissive description of SoBL's presentation of monastic identity as 'very general' is disconcerting, at the very least.

Rees writes that in the general chapter of 1969 the EBC set up a Commission on the Theology of the Monastic Life

> with the purpose of drafting a document that would make explicit those theological principles and particular emphases which lie behind our own Congregation's manner of conceiving the monastic life and indicate how they can be pointers for its future.[13]

He further notes that 'it was still intended at that time to blend this theological statement with the Constitutions which were being revised concurrently', which appears to have been the intention of *Ecclesiae Sanctae* on this point. However, this manner of proceeding was not found workable by the EBC monks and nuns tasked with the responsibility of progressing the document of theological principles. Rees explains:

---

[13] Rees, *Consider Your Call*, p. xiii.

the [Theology] Commission soon objected that a theological investigation could hardly be pursued if it had to shape itself to a predetermined juridical framework, and urged that the two processes of theological reflection and canonical revision be carried out independently of one another.[14]

The objectors carried the day, and what Rees (in a telling phrase) terms the Commission's 'plea for autonomy' was accepted by the authorities of the EBC, with the result that revision of the Congregation's constitutions was carried forward independently of the 'theological investigation' being pursued by the Commission, this latter being the process that produced *Consider Your Call*.

Rees notes that this manner of proceeding 'does not necessarily preclude any eventual interaction between their document [i.e. *Consider Your Call*] and the new Constitutions'.[15] In practice, however, no such 'interaction' has ever taken place, and it is surely open to question whether such an approach was either necessary or useful in the first place.[16] Why, for example, need it be the case that 'concurrent' development of a theological statement of monastic identity and a set of congregational constitutions should result in a 'predetermined juridical framework' being imposed upon the work of the theologians? At the same time, it can be asked whether the process ultimately adopted by the EBC, which drove a wedge between theological reflection and juridical formulation, was in practice a fulfilment either of the injunctions of *Ecclesiae Sanctae* or of the intentions of SoBL. One commentator on *Consider Your Call* from another Benedictine congregation is explicit in his view that 'the document that presents the "theological principles" contains

---

[14] Ibid., p. xiv.

[15] The 1969 constitutions, meanwhile, were revised independently of the theological labours of the CYC team, in a process which extended from 1981 to 1986, incorporating the new Code of Canon Law of 1983. They were approved by the EBC general chapter in 1985 and confirmed by the Holy See in 1986.

[16] Luke Beckett, *The Canonical Understanding of Spiritual Leadership in Religious Life* (Rome: Pontifical University of Saint Thomas Aquinas, 2011), p. 233.

material that should appear in a Constitution or a Customary', and from today's perspective it is difficult not to agree.[17]

Arguably, by failing to carry forward the theological and juridical processes together, establishing instead what was effectively a two-track approach to the renewal of monastic identity, the Congregation weakened each track of its road to renewal. The status of the EBC theological statement was thereby rendered ambiguous. Despite being the outcome of the congregational process described above, and being launched publicly at Westminster Cathedral in May 1978 by the President of the Congregation as a text that 'represents the EBC's post-conciliar rethought statement on Monasticism',[18] *Consider Your Call* says of itself:

> Although this book has been written under the patronage of the EBC, none of the views here expressed should be taken to reflect that Congregation's official and final standpoint. We hope, however, that our investigations have been pursued in the spirit which animates the Congregation, one of freedom combined with care for inherited responsibilities.[19]

In other words, the text has no actual standing within the monasteries of the EBC. If the book does not represent an 'official' standpoint, one might ask, to what end is it to be used within the monasteries of the EBC? One notes also in this passage a renewed concern about issues of autonomy ('freedom'), which may perhaps once again signal a desire to play down any sense that the book is an 'official' statement. Is a concern to address what we have seen Casey term 'evident tradition' as the heart of monastic identity adequately conveyed (or, indeed, intended) by the expression 'care for inherited responsibilities'? This latter expression might perhaps more comfortably find a place in the mission statement of the National Trust than of a Benedictine congregation.

---

[17] Ambrose Wathen, 'Consider Your Call, Considered', in *The American Benedictine Review*, 30:4 (December 1979), p. 361.

[18] *The Ampleforth Journal*, Autumn 1978, p. 22.

[19] Rees, *Consider Your Call*, p. xv.

As well as the difficulty identified above concerning the status of *Consider Your Call* within the monastic congregation that created it, there is also a tension running through the book in terms of its intended audience. The foreword, written by Cardinal Basil Hume (who – as Abbot Hume – was both a contributor to the book, and a member of the general chapter that commissioned it), insists that the issues discussed in the book are

> issues which concern all Christians today, and indeed all men and women who care for the values on which our society is built … Because the monasticism inspired by St Benedict has traditionally cared for these vital issues, it can speak to the modern world in terms that will not need too much translation.[20]

In summary, what can we say has happened in this post-conciliar process intended to renew the monastic identity of the EBC? We have seen that the EBC has chosen to develop its own congregational statement of monastic identity, in response to both the Council and to the SoBL coming from the Congress of Abbots. Following *Ecclesiae Sanctae*, this statement was intended both to express 'evangelical and theological principles concerning religious life and its incorporation in the Church' and to be 'an apt and accurate formulation in which the spirit and aims of the founder should be clearly recognised and faithfully preserved'.[21] It was to be used to inform the renewed juridical structures of the Congregation through its constitutions. But at an early stage of the process of theological reflection, that process lost any organic connection to the process of juridical renewal in the EBC, and was taken forward without reference to the renewal of the constitutions. Perhaps for this reason, when the book representing the outcome of the congregational theological process was published, the Congregation appeared to have no mechanism available to address that book's status, leaving the text effectively in limbo, as simply *not* the 'official and final standpoint' of the EBC. Finally, *Consider Your Call* is published and presented to the public as a book apparently intended for the general religious reader, with the Cardinal Archbishop of Westminster, himself an

---

[20] Ibid., p. xii.
[21] Ibid., p. xiii.

EBC monk and one of the book's authors, effectively saying as much in the foreword.

Before turning to consider some responses to the book, and to draw conclusions from what has been narrated above, it should be noted here that the agenda urged by Basil Hume's foreword, one in which monasticism was to 'speak to the modern world in terms that will not need too much translation', became increasingly the agenda of the authorities of the EBC after the process which created the book. One year after the appearance of *Consider Your Call*, in 1979, the President of the Congregation asked 'a group of monks and nuns of the EBC ... to write a book drawing on their monastic experience which could be of interest for the lay reader.'[22] The book was to 'communicate the human and spiritual value of the monastic life to others'.

The result was the well-received paperback, *A Touch of God: Eight Monastic Journeys*. This book, which in many respects was the ultimate outcome of the process which began in the EBC as a set of responses to the question of monastic identity, is an explicitly apostolic work, intended to speak from the cloister to lay readers in a contemporary modality, and aiming to illuminate 'the life of every Christian'.[23]

While *Consider Your Call* has largely gathered dust in monastery libraries, *A Touch of God* is remembered positively by many readers of the 1980s and afterwards as a book which influenced them, and itself gave rise to a sequel some thirty years later. I wonder to what extent this seemingly accidental trajectory through theological reflection to apostolic outreach was in fact an accident, and not rather a reflection of unstated aspects of the EBC's self-understanding which need to be articulated and taken seriously as an aspect of its monastic identity?

Before drawing conclusions from this outline account of the making of *Consider Your Call*, I wish to touch briefly on two published reactions to that book, both of them from scholars who are themselves monks.

[22] Maria Boulding, ed., *A Touch of God: Eight Monastic Journeys* (London: SPCK, 1982), p. vii.
[23] Ibid., cover matter.

Writing in the *Ampleforth Journal* soon after the book first appeared, Bishop Christopher Butler finds much to praise in what he terms a 'splendid piece of work'. In a nuanced and insightful review, he nevertheless goes on to suggest that the process which created the book failed to engage with a fundamental issue of Benedictine identity which is especially relevant to the EBC:

> Fundamentally, I suggest, at issue is whether our renewal is to take us back only to the post-Reformation revival of the EBC or, which I think necessary, a recovery of the original inspiration of our sixth-century founder.

Butler finds this issue running through the whole of the text under review. For example, he writes,

> Our authors (eschewing a study of the clericalization of monasticism in the pre-Reformation period) seem, at best, to leave open the question whether renewal should involve a radical declericalization of our Congregation.[24]

This is a telling point, and I shall return to it below.

Significantly, given all that has been said above about appeals in various contexts to issues of 'autonomy', Butler strongly takes issue with the presentation of monastic autonomy in *Consider Your Call*. He writes,

> This means that *essentially* a Benedictine community *must* be outside the control of its local bishop (what would Ignatius of Antioch have thought of that?) and monastic life would be radically undermined if the authority of the local bishop were to be restored.

For Butler, this is to fail 'to take seriously the ecclesiology of the Church as a communion of communions built up around the Eucharist, each local communion looking to its local bishop as the local vicar of Christ', and instead to 'take refuge behind an ideologically biased reading of past history and the enactments of Canon Law'.[25]

---

[24] B. C. Butler, 'Monastic Renewal', *The Ampleforth Journal*, Autumn 1978, p. 27.
[25] Ibid., p. 34.

Butler's is a sympathetic review by an EBC insider. But he is far from uncritical of where his Benedictine brethren have reached in their reflections on monastic identity, and his two key criticisms – that *Consider Your Call* is effectively a study of a post-Reformation monastic movement, and not a 'return to sources', and that the concept of monastic autonomy operative in the book suggests that its authors are, so to speak, ecclesiologically challenged in the post-Vatican II context – are both significant points.

The review by the Swiss-American Benedictine scholar, Ambrose Wathen OSB, is a less sympathetic account, and its author's occasional waspish jibes caused some offence. Two points made by Wathen are of especial significance. The first is his claim that *Consider Your Call* does not deliver as a work of monastic scholarship:

> the book presents itself with all the paraphernalia of a scholarly work. But it falls short of the mark on many counts. The material evidence gained from an analysis of format and mechanics should only caution the reader that the book is not what it pretends to be.

Wathen is not the only reader of this book to ask himself why some of the material in the text is so woefully thin, but his review is, as far as I am aware, the only published statement of this question.

At least equally important is his carefully argued and thought-provoking claim that 'there is an operative model that undergirds much of the theologising found in *Consider Your Call*. That model is *The English Mission* of the post-Reformation.' Wathen explains, 'The authors admit that "monasticism arose in response to no specific apostolic challenge".' But the notion of 'mission' is soon established in chapter three 'The Mission and Relationship of the Church to the World', and it is this universal ecclesial role that seems to place the monastic life in its proper relationship to the world, to the church, and to England in particular.[26]

---

[26] Ambrose Wathen OSB, 'Consider Your Call Considered', 30:4 (1979) pp. 343–69, p. 356.

Wathen argues persuasively that the presentation of monastic life arrived at by the EBC privileges 'mission' over fundamental monastic identity, and indeed reads off the values of the latter in a manner best suited to express and to support the former. He suggests that 'mission' in the EBC context is to be understood in terms of the two goals of the seventeenth-century monks who refounded the Congregation after the dissolution, stated in *Consider Your Call* as:

> First, the establishment of English communities following the Benedictine life, and, second, the conversion of England to the Catholic faith.[27]

In effect, Wathen picks up a part of Butler's critique, presented in outline above, and develops it to its logical conclusion.

Conclusion

This necessarily brief account of a process lasting more than eight years, which resulted in a book running to more than four hundred and fifty pages, is little more than an outline of the former, and has hardly touched at all on the substantive contents of the latter. However, some conclusions about that process and its outcome, which may especially have relevance for any re-engagement in the present moment with the question of monastic identity in the EBC, may be provisionally drawn.

First, one can only agree with Wathen when he says that the undertaking pursued by the authors of *Consider Your Call* is 'a mammoth task'.[28] In saying this, Wathen is concerned with what he calls the historical and contextual 'variables' to be addressed in attempting a theological reflection upon monastic identity. We have seen the Congress of Abbots wrestle with some of these variables in SoBL, and noted there that one of the 'variables' in that context is the status of the Congress itself. Within the local monastic congregation, in this case the EBC, the same difficulty about the status of overarching bodies appears to apply, and

---

[27] Rees, *Consider Your Call*, p. 340.
[28] Wathen, 'Consider Your Call, Considered', p. 364.

Consider Your Call is to some extent the victim of a lack of clarity about the status of the body promulgating it. As we have seen, the book is ultimately not granted any 'official' standing; it is therefore open to question to what extent, even had its contents proven more appealing to its various audiences, it could ever have functioned as a congregational statement of monastic identity for the EBC.

But, secondly, as I have argued above, the early decision to claim theological 'autonomy' from the process of reshaping the constitutions of the Congregation appears to have spectacularly backfired upon its authors, and left the book the theologians wrote with little or no direct purchase upon the life of the monks and nuns for whom it was supposedly written. In making this decision, the EBC arguably impoverished its own internal life by failing to carry through what appear to be the intentions of *Ecclesiae Sanctae*.

Thirdly, as Butler and Wathen each argue in slightly different ways, the model of a (clericalised) monastic mission to the world (or, at least, to England) is the dominant guiding principle running through *Consider Your Call*. As a consequence, a more far-reaching 'return to sources' is precluded. It is this fact about the positions taken up by *Consider Your Call* that appears to me to underlie the book's limitations as a tool for monastic renewal within the EBC, and it is with an elaboration of this point that I shall conclude.

What I earlier termed a trajectory from fundamental theological reflection towards apostolic outreach ('mission' again) in the aim and the intended audience of *Consider Your Call* points towards the following overarching perspective: for the EBC of the post-Vatican II period renewal in monastic life and identity essentially meant renewal of the monastic mission to England, the recalibration of what already existed in order to make it more accessible, perhaps more attractive, to a lay audience, and thus more effective as a tool of monastic mission in modern society. Significantly, it did not mean a substantial recovery of the earlier authentic Benedictine experience, an encounter with the deepened and renewed scholarly return to the sources, or a systematic renewal of institutional structures.

If this analysis has purchase, it may provide a clue to one of the factors that lies behind the 'lack of bite' described at the beginning of this essay. In another context, Robert Barron writes that

> the beige church … went running after modernity, but modernity continued to run away, indifferent to its ardent pursuer.[29]

My suggestion is that something not dissimilar may very possibly have occurred in the monastic context, as the monks and nuns of the Vatican II generation sought what was, effectively, an inculturation of traditional monastic life into European modernity at the very moment when their context was becoming one in which a Christian challenge to the present moment, rather than an accommodation, was the perceived need.

Michael Casey argues that

> one of the endearing qualities of vital monasticism is that, chameleon-like, it tends to take much of its nonessential coloration from its surroundings.

It is a benign statement which of course runs the risk of begging the underlying question of what is and what is not essential to the monastic life. It is for that reason that Casey goes on to point out that, for European monks, making a new monastic foundation in an alien culture presents a challenge:

> it has become hard to determine what belongs to the substance of monastic observance and what is merely local baggage.[30]

Casey's point is that establishing a monastery in a non-European setting forces European monks to decide what is fundamental to monastic life, and what is, by contrast, simply European colouration or local baggage. It also plunges such a community into dialogue with the potentially challenging critique of their new, non-European brethren, who will naturally have their own ideas on the subject.

Perhaps this is the same challenge that faces the monks and nuns of traditional monastic congregations in Europe and

---

[29] Barron, 'The Depressing Pew Forum Study'.
[30] Casey, 'Thoughts', p. 33.

America: how in effect to refound their existing communities within the culture of their own post-Christian society in such a way that the full vitality of the gospel and the monastic tradition can be discovered in their way of living.

Reflection Questions

1. What do you understand by the term 'loss of bite' here? Do you think this has happened to religious life? If so, in what way?

2. The problem of identity in religious life has been discussed for decades. What do you understand this to be about?

3. Why does the author think *A Touch of God* was so much more successful than *Consider Your Call*? How does this chapter help you to consider the history of your own congregation's policies of adaptation and renewal since the Council?

3

Some Reflections on the Religious Brothers' Vocation since Vatican II: Its Present and Future

Benedict Foy FSC

Introduction

Writing this chapter I am conscious of the generalised nature of my reflections. Do I try to write about religious brothers in general? Do I differentiate between the 'professional-type brothers': qualified teachers, nurses, social workers, as opposed to the 'lay-brother type', usually found humbly working at manual tasks within clerical congregations, amongst whom I count two of my own relatives? For authenticity's sake I will focus on the 'professional-type religious brother', which is my own life experience. I see a great diversity between individual brothers, and between the different brothers' communities, whether at local, national or international level, all of whom are committed to live as religious brothers. Consequently, I will write from the personal perspective of an English De La Salle brother, with a background in education and retreat work, who has had some involvement with other brothers' congregations in recent years, and whose experience of religious life almost exactly corresponds to Vatican II and its reception over the last fifty years.

I became a novice in 1963, shortly after the opening of Vatican II. So I have lived as a religious brother through the whole fifty years since Vatican II. Although as novices we compiled scrapbooks of reports about the Council, our formation, as in other brothers' congregations, was a strictly pre-conciliar one, almost monastic in form and content, 'pietistic, impersonal and conformative', as one brother described it to me recently. It followed the classical model of preparing people to live seeking for 'a state of perfection'. Ideals were based on a traditional scriptural theology like, 'be ye perfect as your heavenly father is perfect' or 'the harvest is great and the labourers are few'. If anything, the typical formation reflected a dualist-type of understanding of the religious vocation of a brother, a split between being holy and being a person. Our own personal salvation was to be our first aim. Mission and ministry, which were the very reasons which attracted most of us to the brother's vocation, were poor seconds to this preoccupation. Yet there was little expectation or preparation to encounter God personally. The training in mental prayer was mainly a mechanism of using various acts of devotion, employing the correct kind of abstract theological phrases seemed to be the ideal. The spirituality of our founder, rarely specifically alluded to, was fundamentally apophatic in form.

Two or three years later, whilst still students, we started to become aware of brothers leaving in significant numbers. About the same time, as a consequence of the renewal chapter of 1966/7, we became aware of striking changes in how our vocation was being spoken of and written about. The directives of the Vatican Council mandated renewal and adaptation of all groups in religious life, based on the study of scripture, on a return to the origins of their institute and on an appropriate adaptation to the world. This became a source of great interest and excitement for us as young brothers. The new English Mass and a greater sensitivity to world issues contributed to our heightened expectations at this time.

Prior to the Council

In 1956 an appreciation of the new kind of world following World War II at last became apparent to the general chapter of the De La Salle Brothers. The previous chapter in 1946 had attempted to 'return to normality', regardless of the radical changes in the world and the searing impact of the disruptions caused to the lives and mission of the brothers during the war. Belatedly recognising the changed world and the challenges to the brothers' vocation in 1956, two significant decisions were made which were, in hindsight, particularly providential.

The first decision was to establish a serious study of the life of our founder and the origins of the Institute to better understand the nature of the brothers' vocation. Study and much wider dissemination of our founder's writings were undertaken, and especially of certain seminal texts that previously had hardly been accessible because they did not match what had become a monastic outlook. The texts that had been put to one side were not of the prescriptive, regulatory kind but reflected much that was inspirational and foundational. They have now been restored to their rightful place.

The second joint decision of the teaching brothers' congregations was to establish in Rome an institute for advanced theological studies for brothers, the Jesus Magister Institute, attached to one of the Roman universities. It was soon realised that many of the brothers were likely to achieve better degrees than priestly students. Nevertheless a class distinction held sway. Proctors told brothers defending their doctoral theses, 'Because you are only brothers you will have to wait to let the priest-candidates go first', despite having been scheduled by alphabetical order.

The Council

Several of the brothers trained at Jesus Magister, became *periti* at the Council. The superior general of the De La Salle Brothers, as the leader of the largest non-clerical, male teaching congregation, was an official observer at the Council. Through these factors, and because of the hospitality given in the general houses of various brothers' congregations to many third-world Council fathers and others, throughout the Council, religious brothers based in Rome were very aware of the thinking and decisions of the Council.

John O'Malley SJ, an historian of Vatican II, at a lecture in Oxford in 2011, characterised changes resulting from Vatican II as follows:

> from laws to ideals, from commands to invitations, from threats to persuasion, from ruling to serving, from rivalry to partnership,

from hostility to friendship, from fault-finding to seeking common ground, from suspicion to trust, from passive acceptance to active participation, from rules to conscience, from behaviour modification to conversion of heart.

Overwhelmingly, religious brothers accepted these as gifts of the Holy Spirit and adopted the opportunities which it offered to live prophetically and creatively in a changing world, though perhaps not to the same extent as the religious sisters. But since Vatican II the life of religious brothers can also be characterised by various tensions, changes and movements. The following are some of the more significant, each of which could be considered as a spectrum depending on the brother or his congregation.

- Vatican II's focus on 'local churches' against the 'universal perspectives' of religious congregations.

- The universal call to holiness and religious living in 'a state of perfection'.

- A dualistic-type of self-concept to an integrated incarnational sense.

- Being responsible for ministries to being partners (even minor or marginal ones) in ministries.

- 'Carrying the charism' and 'sharing the charism' of the congregations.

- Being self-sufficient or self-contained or being collaborative, and accountable.

- The expectations of the institutional church; issues of subsidiarity; new societal demands.

- Understanding and living out of the vows in an increasing secular, materialistic, multicultural, multifaith plurivalent and laissez-faire world.

- Abstract theological discussion or experiential reflection/revelation of God in all things.

- Ecclesial authority and theology as against an Incarnational theology and practical salvation.

Some Tensions between the Institutional church and brothers
arising from Vatican II

During their chapter of 1966/7 the De La Salle Brothers prepared
A Declaration: The Brothers of the Christian Schools in the World Today.
The document outlined for the brothers

> the continual call to be prayerful and attentive to the Holy Spirit,
> and a call to commit ourselves again to the poor.

It also recognised the significant involvement of lay colleagues in
the mission, a great change since the 1946 general chapter which
saw them as 'a necessary evil'. Paradoxically, both the De La Salle
Brothers and the Marist Brothers, in their first post-Vatican II
general chapters 1966/67, experienced significant interference
from the then Prefect and Secretary of the Congregation for
Religious. Both attempted to exert intense pressure on these
brothers' congregations, and possibly on others, to accept the
privilege and 'gift of ordination' offered as an option by the
Council, displaying a complete lack of recognition or respect for
the history and traditions of both of these congregations. The
pressure also took the form of attempted interference in the
elections of the superiors general, contrary to the congregations'
rules, and of insisting that their comments in favour of priestly
ordination be publically recorded and widely published. This did
little to commend the acceptance of the priesthood to the brothers,
the votes for which were resoundingly negative. An appeal to the
Vatican Commission for the Interpretation of Vatican II upheld
the brothers' understandings. This is a small but telling vignette
of the tensions which continue to exist between the clerical church
and the brothers' self-understanding and identity; between the
clerical model involving prestige, power and control and the
brothers' prophetic witness to experiencing Jesus in community,
ministry and simplicity. Another brother relates that at a public
conference about this time a priest speaker said that religious
brothers

> could come closer to the heart of Holy Mother Church if they
> were at least ordained deacons.

Some orders of brothers did accept that some members might become priests but this has largely been an unhappy experience.

The universal call to holiness and service by Vatican II was perceived by some brothers as an undervaluing and undermining of their commitment to living in a state of perfection, which hopefully would virtually guarantee them heaven. Since Vatican II it seems as if support by the institutional church for non-clerical religious life has diminished. Very rarely have I ever heard public prayer offered specifically for brothers' vocations. The Vatican's apparent preference in recent years is for the 'new ecclesial communities' and a lack of recognition of the contribution of religious over the years seems to be the norm in recent pontificates. This perception was explicitly acknowledged in February 2010 by Cardinal Rode, then Prefect of the Dicastery for Consecrated Life.

A Christian Brother recently wrote,

> Maybe this is part of the meaning of being brother, to serve and not to be served, to accept the lowest place. As brothers we don't seek power, control or status.[1]

However, many brothers abandoned their religious vocation, especially those in teaching congregations: a comment perhaps not just on the church's devaluing of the brothers' vocation, but also perhaps reflecting society's views of the teaching profession. Many of those who left have lived good and committed lives within the married state and in lay ministry, and often maintain warm links with their former confrères, though that has mostly developed in the last twenty years. It may well be the case that former brothers (and their wives) now feel more comfortable because the brothers feel that they have less that they must defend.

A particular stress for brothers arising from Vatican II is the awareness that the Council promoted, at least theoretically, the importance of the local church, under the leadership of the local bishop. Especially for members of exempt congregations, a

---

[1] Quote taken from private correspondence.

somewhat schizophrenic attitude developed.[2] As religious, our perspective is often national or inter-national and is not limited to a particular parish, diocese or country. The importance of and commitment to their own communities and ministries also tends to turn the brothers' focus of attention inward rather than to the local church situation. I vividly remember a senior priest, now bishop, telling me that he was happy to see me, a brother, 'come down off the mountain and take a significant responsibility in the local church' for the Papal Visit in 1982. The fact that this was done over and above my regular full-time ministry meant that my community's support and understanding was sometimes stretched. Despite being good friends with the priest, I have always felt that his comment betrayed a lack of understanding of the commitment of a brother. The need for dialogue and understanding is still important.

The presence of God and identity

Since this time I and many brothers have learned, as Jack Mahoney SJ commented, to make faith-sense of experience and experience-sense of faith. To recognise and experience God not simply in the sacraments, Eucharist or scriptures but also in the difficult student, or the drunken person, or the seriously disturbed patient is a glorious reality in brothers' lives. This is further enhanced by the conviction that we are called to be God's ambassadors to bring the Good News to the same people, wherever they are, offering practical salvation. This reciprocal relationship precisely is the deeply incarnational theological perspective of the brothers' vocation. It reflects the relational realities of the Trinity, the incarnational fraternal reality of Jesus and the constant presence and action of the Spirit. Our spirituality, especially since Vatican II, has become a positive, cataphatic one, a spirituality tuned in to life, a spirituality which, quoting G. M. Hopkins, 'sees deep down things'.

---

[2] Religious congregations under the direct authority of a general superior, rather than that of a local bishop.

The abstract theologies of other ecclesial perspectives on vocation simply do not, for me, touch the lived experience of 'being brother'. Ours is an integrated view of life where the holy is experienced within the everyday details of life and where 'being brother' and 'brothering' are coterminous with our sense of identity. Brothers are not part of the hierarchical structure nor of the sacramental service of the church but we share in the work of evangelisation by our loving practical action in the everyday lives of people and, as such, like all members of the church, we are part of the sacramental structure of the church. As ministers of the Word we sometimes even use words to touch the hearts of those we minister to and with. As part of the brothers' identity we recognise that we are increasingly becoming one with Jesus, our brother. This close identification with Jesus enables brothers to stand alongside people, especially those suffering and most in need, and in this way to help transform their pain to joy, their suffering to new life, to be part of Jesus' redemptive actions. It was precisely this holding of people's sufferings that Fr Christopher Jamison OSB, then Abbot of Worth, has identified as that which distinguished him, a monk, from religious brothers. Maybe this reflects the following excerpt from *Vita Consecrata*:

> Consecrated persons discover that the more they stand at the foot of the Cross of Christ, the more immediate and profoundly they experience the truth of God who is love.[3]

After Vatican II a considerable number of brothers left religious life. Most brothers who stayed have gained a deeper sense of their vocation, as being continuously called to live out their baptismal commitment through their consecration as religious brothers and by being part of a ministering community.

The experience of community
The experience of community has certainly changed since Vatican II, mainly through some more contemporary and relevant insights into the Trinity. Schillebeeckx commented that

---

[3] *Vita Consecrata*, 24.

70

a democratic form [of governance] is a better ... model for creating a church in which the Spirit's impulse can be expressed by all.[4]

This is definitely the model experienced today in brothers' communities: it is more respectful and fraternal. Community prayer prior to Vatican II was usually a recital of 'indulgenced' prayers of previous generations which had little to do with the world in which brothers found themselves or their life experiences. Despite the shortcomings of formation, many brothers maintained and developed a committed life of prayer. In the years after Vatican II many brothers found new ways of praying. Community prayer became more varied, according to the preferences and experiences of the community. Prayer for the needs of those we minister with and to whom we minister grounds the reflection, meditation and sharing of brothers in a way which enhances their ministerial commitment. The deeper consequential awareness of God in the lives and ministry of brothers is shared and celebrated in a manner which is much more natural, relevant and coherent than the old formulaic prayers.

Loss and spreading of charisms
For those brothers who have remained after Vatican II there has often been an increased sense of diminishment and pain, both from the loss of good men with whom they had spent years of their lives and from the loss of large communities which sustained them in their youthful experience of ministry, exacerbated by the non-appearance of new members and the ageing of the rest. Gone too are the big, often prestigious, institutions for which they were responsible and in which many of them had dedicated their lives, increasingly taken over by lay colleagues. While some brothers found these changes very difficult, others came to see the increasing number of lay

---

[4] Daniel Speed Thompson, *The Language of Dissent: Edward Schillebeeckx on the Crisis of Authority in the Catholic Church* (Notre Dame, IN: University of Notre Dame Press, 2003), p. 160.

colleagues as a sign of success and empowerment of others. Other brothers are happy that they are no longer seen as controllers or enforcers of discipline in institutions but are freer to witness to the love and care of God, to witness to the 'fraternal' relationships of the Trinity as part of their congregation's charism or spirit, seeing that these charisms, whether in education, nursing or social care, do not belong just to their own congregation but are the gift of the Holy Spirit to the church as a whole. Many brothers today, and certainly more than before Vatican II, share the charism of their congregations (e.g. faith and zeal of the De La Salle Congregation or hospitality of the Hospitallers of John of God) and their resultant faith experiences, both within their com-munities and within the wider community of the church.

The concern of most congregations in recent years has been to share their charism, to pass it on and to develop their 'spiritual capital', with their lay colleagues and successors. This cannot be to attempt to create 'mini-brothers' amongst lay colleagues who include men and women, Catholics and many faiths and none, and all styles of life. The efforts in the formation, or awakening and deepening the spiritual awareness of lay colleagues, are directed at inviting collaborators to recognise God's presence in their lives and ministries, and to share God's love with those they are ministering alongside by being reflective about what and how they minister.

The demands of government regulation, the expectations of public accountability and the impact of a secular and pluralist culture in the professional fields of ministry are often perceived as threatening the religious and spiritual purposes of brothers' former establishments, making the demand for the formation of colleagues even more urgent, and is something which many lay associates themselves are looking for. Brothers' congregations are committing significant portions of their diminishing resources to self-evaluation of the ethos of institutions as well as the professional aspects of their ministries.

In Great Britain the first generation of lay successors to brothers as head teachers is complete, yet the development of the schools continues apace. Cooperation and collaboration between schools, nationally and internationally, has spread while staff and students are increasingly involved in actions of solidarity on behalf of the world's most needy within their own schools' localities and internationally, under the banner of 'enter to learn, leave to serve'. The lay heads themselves are expressing concerns about continuing the brothers' or even Catholic ethos of their schools in the light of multicultural and multifaith school admissions, and are actively seeking new ways to address this issue. Because many heads consider the brothers to be 'the heart, memory and guarantors of the Lasallian Mission' they are increasingly turning to brothers to help them in the formation in spiritual awareness of their staffs. This is a new form of the brothers' ministry of education for today. A similar commitment exists of the Hospitaller Brothers of St John of God to the formation of their burgeoning number of lay colleagues in the field of health care.

Commitment and consecration

Some congregations of brothers, or some provinces of other congregations, have disappeared since Vatican II. Some may say that this is part of the normal life cycle of religious congregations.[5] Others suggest that these disappearances are consequences of abandoning the traditional elements of religious life like loss of a prayer life, no longer wearing the habit, living outside of community, changing apostolates or the adoption of individual, secular or materialistic values. While there have been examples of these changes since Vatican II, these also appeared for a variety of reasons long before Vatican II, often as a result of wars and revolutions. But this is not the reality for most brothers' congregations.

My experience over the years since Vatican II suggests that brothers' understanding and living out of their vowed commitment has been much more positive. This has led to a more mature and humanly integrated living of the religious vows.

---

[5] cf. Raymond Hostie, *The Life and Death of Religious Orders* (Washington: Center for the Applied Research in the Apostolate (CARA), 1983).

The shadow of recent years

Tragically the experience of addictions, abuse and cover-ups has become more evident in recent years and has affected some brothers' congregations more than others, and some parts of the world more than others. From a psychological perspective I consider that such addictions are the very antithesis of a true spirituality. These difficulties experienced by brothers are ways they have developed for coping with the gap between the ideals by which they wanted to live their lives and the lived realities they were attempting to cope with. I don't believe that levels of addiction or abuse are any worse since Vatican II than before. They have always existed in society and in the church. I suspect that the dualistic understanding of religious life before Vatican II made some contribution to the problems.

The situation of recent years reflects the greater transparency required of the church and of religious congregations. The brothers' congregations in Great Britain have recently been in the vanguard of working to improve safeguarding measures which include far more effective vetting of candidates, greater sensitivity to possibilities and strong and effective means to deal with potential difficulties.

Today

Presently there are about fifty thousand religious brothers worldwide, of whom some four thousand are De La Salle Brothers, collaborating with about ninety thousand teachers, more than half of whom are women. Recognising that more than half of those who today share the Lasallian spirit are women is a highly significant post-conciliar shift and one which will surely have a major impact for how the spirit of St John Baptist de La Salle will be lived out in the future. We, De La Salle Brothers, are associated together to accompany about one million young people in over eighty countries, of many ethnicities, cultures and faiths, to offer them a human and Christian or spiritual education, whether in universities, in mission countries, in pastoral and retreat centres for the young or in the printed and electronic word, whilst our 'core mission' of work for existing schools continues.

Today, a number of congregations of religious sisters follow the spirituality and mission of St John Baptist de La Salle. Founded in Mexico, Haiti, in Vietnam and Thailand, they work increasingly closely with the brothers. A secular institute, the Catechists of Jesus Crucified, founded by an Italian De La Salle brother, also works closely with the brothers in a number of countries. Elsewhere groups of lay people, after a serious formation in Lasallian Spirituality, make promises to commit themselves to voluntary support for education work with young people in need. After over three hundred years existence of the De La Salle Brothers, there still is an obvious need for the Lasallian charism to continue.

The future and a new perspective

Since Vatican II the number of religious brothers globally has halved, in the USA diminishing at a rate of 66%. In developing countries there are some significant numbers of new members. Here the challenge is to form them in the charisms of the various institutes whilst coping with different cultural expectations which these new recruits bring with them. The various ministries of the brothers' congregations are still very much needed in developing countries even if the state has taken over the services the brothers' congregations used to provide in many 'first-world' countries. But even within our own country, the need for people to 'brother others' remains in a cultural situation where people are becoming ever more isolated and lonely. To 'be brother' is, I think, becoming more important than what we specifically do as brothers. As brothers we are learning increasingly to live with ambiguity.

At the general chapter of 2007 an event occurred which I consider to be highly significant for the future of the De La Salle Brothers' Congregation and the Lasallian charism, one which takes us (precisely in the spirit of Vatican II) back to our original inspiration, and one which may have validity for brothers' and sisters' congregations in general. For the first forty years of the life of the Brothers' Institute, the brothers pronounced three vows: association for the mission of education, especially of the poor, stability or commitment to live in community to facilitate this ministry and obedience. They did not take the traditional three vows of poverty, chastity and obedience, though in fact they lived these evangelical counsels which were implicit in their Rule. Conditional for reception of the church's approbation the brothers had to accept the three traditional vows. Although the preface for the new Rule of 1725 suggested that taking these vows was a privilege, it did in fact fundamentally change the understanding of the nature of the brothers' vocation. I believe that it was this change which was the basic cause of the dualistic attitude which affected the brothers' identity for over two hundred years. Certainly, it significantly undermined De La Salle's consistent teaching about prayer and recognising God's presence in every situation and in everyone. His teaching had pointed to letting the brothers see that their ministry (a word that he used long before it came into general use in the church), although a lay ministry, not a monastic-type vocation, was a sharing in Jesus' mission which in turn shaped how they lived their religious life.

Following approval in 1725 the understanding of the brothers' mission was thus arbitrarily changed, now being shaped by the imposed framework of religious life. For over two hundred years a tension existed about the proper understanding the brothers' vocation. In fact association virtually disappeared as the consolidating principle of the De La Salle Brothers' vocation.

It was only resolved at the 2007 general chapter as a result of the Lasallian studies on our origins, through a greater emphasis in recent years on association (which included our lay colleagues), and following the intervention of Br John Johnston, the former superior general. This led chapter members to reformulate the vows in line with the 1718 formula and the original inspiration for making vows. They were also able to persuade the church authorities to accept this change in conformity with Vatican II's guidelines for renewal. Recovery of the primary importance of the vow of association for mission and the primacy it gives to understanding the brothers' ministry-based vocation has opened a new era and light for the understanding and development of the De La Salle Brothers' sense of vocation. I suspect that the principle has significance for the understanding of vocation in other brothers' congregations and of the vocation of religious sisters.

In the light of this recovery I wonder whether a further custom of the brothers might also be restored. For over two hundred years we had a tradition of 'novice-employees' who were men that, for whatever reason, only ever made annual vows or even no vows at all, but who lived their lives as brothers, alongside those who made perpetual vows. When the 1917 Code of Canon Law was imposed, without consultation, we lost over eight hundred of these brothers at a stroke. I am aware of some people today looking at making commitments at different levels and for longer or shorter periods to live alongside brothers and other religious. Perhaps the model is there to be revisited already.

Conclusion

Since Vatican II we are living in a greatly changed, globalised world where cyber-technology permits almost immediate and uncontrolled access to global information, views and attitudes. In this kind of world, institutions which rely on tradition, secrecy, continuity, predictability, certainty and control have a difficult time. Consequently, a tension exists in brothers' congregations, and even more so within the institutional church itself, between fidelity to the past and adaptability to be able effectively to minister God's love in the constantly changing needs of our world. Recently a former provincial of the Christian Brothers wrote that as brothers being set apart from the clerical and hierarchical structures we are prophetically 'free to oppose anything contrary to the will of God and to speak the truth in love'. A similar theme underlies the recent book of Br Louis DeThomasis FSC, *Flying in the Face of Tradition: Listening to the Lived Experience of the Faithful*.[6]

Will the brothers' congregations die out as a category of religious life? I don't think so, at least not in the immediate future.

---

[6] Louis DeThomasis FSC, *Flying in the Face of Tradition: Listening to the Lived Experience of the Faithful* (Chicago: ACTA Publications, 2012).

But I consider that is the practical consequence of the New Testament injunction of *metanoia* to keep on changing. Being free of hierarchical structures frees us from clerical concerns. A Christian Brother recently wrote,

> The Brother's vocation prophetically calls him to an ever-new daily experience of God, whose ways are always beyond what we can imagine, and yet who is active in every choice for life that confronts us today.[7]

I can easily envisage a future that includes collaborative ministry, with the support of brothers from other countries, from other similar congregations, or with committed lay colleagues. Those who point to an inevitable extinction of brothers' congregations forget that the De La Salle Congregation has previously faced extinction at the time of the French Revolution and in 1904, when over four thousand brothers were forced to leave their schools in Paris alone, not to mention elsewhere in France. In the future it may well be seen that this post-Vatican II epoch may be considered as another round of the pruning required for good organic growth, returning in strength after adapting (not without pain) to new situations. This is not to suggest a false sense of complacency, but the charisms of the brothers' congregations are the gifts of God's Spirit to the whole church, through which God will provide for the needs of God's people. As brothers we simply want to remain faithful to God's will, whether we remain as religious brothers or whether the charism is completely carried by lay people. We are, in the words of Newman, 'links in the chain' of God's mission, 'simply to be used'.[8]

The experience of religious fraternity, after the experience of consecrated widows and virgins, has been the longest lasting of the forms of religious life in the church, which would make its

---

[7] Quote taken from private correspondence.

[8] See John Henry Newman, 'Meditations on Christian Doctrine with A Visit to the Blessed Sacrament Before Meditation', *The National Institute for Newman Studies: Newman Reader* [website]
<http://www.newmanreader.org/works/meditations/meditations9.html>

complete disappearance highly unlikely. The radical witness of men who can live together as brothers in intentional communities because of their common belief in God has an increasing significance for a world suffering fragmentation.

The increasing collaboration of women has given new insights into the fraternal lives and ministries of religious brothers, providing a new sense of balance and sensitivity in relationships, and marking a new stage and sense of the inclusivity of the development of the Lasallian charism and ministry. It stands as a prophetic witness to the institutional church to assist it to become more inclusive and relevant in our world. A constant struggle I have had in writing this chapter is to find words which adequately express what I understand about the religious vocation. Words like: charism, vocation, formation, salvation, sacrifice, vowed commitment, faith and zeal, although they may be understood by 'professional religious' and the institutional church, are difficult to express in a meaningful manner as a result of the changing understandings of our world.

To be able to call someone 'brother' and mean it, whatever their colour, nationality or faith, gives hope for the possibility of collaboration and peace for all. For adults who can be brothers to young people, for carers who can brother the most forsaken, for men who can brother whoever they meet, simply because they know that they themselves are brothers of Jesus, who has committed himself to them and to whom they have committed themselves, is a powerful sign of God's love in our world.

We brothers might individually and collectively have regrets that what has given us life so far may not continue, or that there are no clear signposts for the future. But what remains for us is hope: not optimism, but trust in God's providence. That leaves religious brothers free to do what we believe God still wants of us: giving and receiving God's love and grace whoever we are with, knowing that as we do so, we are encountering and sharing Jesus, our brother. Is this not what *Lumen Gentium* asks of us?

Religious should carefully consider that, through them, to believers and non-believers alike, the Church truly wishes to give an increasingly clear witness of Christ. Through them Christ should be shown contemplating on the mountainside, announcing God's kingdom to the multitude, healing the sick and the maimed, turning sinners to wholesome fruit, blessing children, doing good to all, and always obeying the will of the Father who sent Him.[9]

What more could we ask for?

Reflection Questions

1. The author describes the effect on his congregation of renewed research into the original writings of the founder. Why do you think the Council urged religious to 'return to sources' and what effect did this have in the experience of your congregation?

2. Why did the brothers resist calls from curial authorities to become ordained? Do you think they were right to do so, and if so, why? What is the significance for the church of having male religious who are not priests?

3. The author speaks of passing on the order's ethos or 'spiritual capital' to lay people? Have you had any experience of this within your own congregation? How has it been done, and to what effect?

---

[9] *Lumen Gentium*, 46.

4

Aspects of Mission in Religious Life since the Second Vatican Council

Vivienne Keely CHF

An analysis of the responses to the *Lineamenta* for *Vita Consecrata*, processed through the Union of International Superiors General (UISG) set the contours for this chapter on mission for apostolic religious congregations. The responses were described as honest and balanced, acknowledging both the light and shadows of mission in the lives of religious.[1] On the positive side, a large number of respondents affirmed a deeper understanding of the fundamental unity between consecration and mission, the importance of context in mission, a greater awareness of the ecclesial dimension of religious life, its prophetic role in the church, and the option for the poor. Also affirmed was the necessity of collaboration with lay people. On the shadow side, the strained relations between groups within the church drew comment from many respondents. This chapter will focus on four aspects of mission drawn from the above responses: thinking about mission; the changing context for mission; the prophetic role of religious; ecclesial tensions. Soundings will be taken from *Lumen Gentium*, *Perfectae Caritatis*, *Vita Consecrata* and the 2012 Synod on the New Evangelisation.[2] It is indeed difficult to conceive of talking seriously about the mission of religious in the

---

[1] Marguerite Letourneau, 'The Consecrated life and its Role in the Church and the World: An Overview of Responses to the *Vita Consecrata*', in *Synodal Perspectives* (UISG, 1994), no. 4, 9–18.

[2] Congregation for Institutes of Consecrated Life and Societies of Apostolic Life, *Consecrated Life in the Third Millennium: Starting Afresh from Christ* (2002), 3.

present day without considering the collaboration of religious with lay people, and the various movements which associate themselves with the charism of particular institutes, but the inclusion of these perspectives is beyond the scope of this chapter.

Mission is a word which is much bandied about. Significant sums of money have been spent worldwide by organisations to create mission statements, and later, to revise, enhance and rewrite those very same statements. Nevertheless, businesses, governments and not-for-profit organisations understand clearly the importance of mission statements in their attempts to distil and promote the purposes of their respective organisations. The personnel in these organisations decide what their mission is and the statement serves to articulate it to the organisation and other interested parties. However, mission in religious life, mission in the church, is radically different because it is neither self-determined nor chapter-directed. Mission is grounded in the gospel,

> God so loved the world that he gave his only Son so that everyone who believes in him might not perish but might have eternal life.
>
> *John 3:16*

This act of giving is God's intervention in human history, the insertion of the Word incarnate in the world, and the mission of God is that we might have life through his son, Jesus. Thus the first movement is one of love, God's love. And we who 'have come to know and to believe in the love God has for us' (1 John 4:16) share in God's mission by helping people to realise that God loves them and shows his love in sending Jesus, the permanent priority for mission.[3] The primacy of love is stressed in Benedict XVI's second encyclical, *Spe Salvi*, where he asserts that the only thing that is truly indestructible is love.[4] Therefore, an essential task of mission is to help people recover, or become aware of, their sense of being a person loved by God. This is the

---

[3] Congregation for Institutes of Consecrated Life and Societies of Apostolic Life, Post-Synodal Apostolic Exhortation, *Vita Consecrata* (1996), 79.

[4] Benedict XVI, *Spe Salvi*, 35.

mission of God, and was the ministry and example of Christ, the missionary of the Father.[5]

The seminal document of the Second Vatican Council, *Lumen Gentium*, in its chapter on religious, concerned itself primarily with the evangelical counsels, the eschatological witness of the counsels, and relations between religious and bishops. It asserted the authority of the hierarchy 'to govern, with wise legislation, the practice of the evangelical counsels'.[6] *Perfectae Caritatis* distinguished between contemplative orders and apostolic congregations, and the activities proper to each. In enjoining communities to engage in renewal, *Perfectae Caritatis* referred to their contemporary mission in the church and the high regard in which those who profess the evangelical counsels are held.[7] The concept of perfection is central to its thinking on religious life. Religious enthusiastically embarked on the renewal called for in *Perfectae Caritatis* and, in particular, on the rediscovery or emphasis on the original charism of the institute but, in this exercise, it seems that thinking on mission itself was subordinated to rediscovery of the charism, an endeavour which, in some cases, created, or augmented, existing ecclesial tensions.

Vita Consecrata, appearing in 1996, was much more explicit in its references to the mission of religious, declaring that 'consecrated life is at the very heart of the church as a decisive element for her mission'. Religious are deemed to be 'in mission by virtue of their consecration'.[8] This notion of mission is reflected in the statement of the UISG Theological Reflection Group,

> Sharing in this mission of Jesus and the Holy Spirit, being sent to the world which God loves is the very axis of our life. Our mission consists essentially not in what we do but in being sent to extend God's reign in creation and in the world.[9]

---

[5] *Vita Consecrata*, 22.

[6] *Lumen Gentium*, 46.

[7] *Perfectae Caritatis*, 7, 8, 25.

[8] *Vita Consecrata*, 3, 23, 25, 72.

[9] UISG Theological Reflection Group, 'Theological Reflection on our Thirty Year Post-Conciliar Experience of Feminine Apostolic Religious Life', in *Synodal Perspectives* (UISG, 1994), no. 94, 22.

The same emphases are taken up in the *Starting Afresh from Christ*, which appeared five years after *Vita Consecrata*, and was an attempt to consider the effectiveness with which *Vita Consecrata* had been received and implemented. Affirmations include the teaching that consecration places religious in mission and that an authentic consecrated life is shown by zeal for the Kingdom of God. The unity of purpose between renewal and mission is identified.[10] The role of religious in the *missio Dei* is clearly stated, 'the proclamation of Christ to all is a task that falls especially to consecrated men and women', and is linked to several calls to expressing this mission primarily among the poor, in activity related to the dignity of the human person, the traditional areas of education and health services and the then newer loci of ecumenical, inter-religious dialogues and ecological questions.[11]

The understanding of mission and the mission of religious since the Second Vatican Council has been both extended and refined. The great gift of *Lumen Gentium* was the teaching that as all are called to holiness, so all participate in the mission of God. Therefore the proclamation of Christ is the task of every baptised person. The universal call to holiness brought with it an emerging sense of the universal call to mission as an obligation of our common baptism. Another major shift was to be found in the integration of mission *ad gentes* with the overall mission of the church such that one could hardly envisage a new church Council issuing a separate document on missions. Advances in psychology and other human sciences have sharpened the awareness of the importance of developing the whole person and resulted in changed and enriched policies and practices for formation of religious for mission. Inculturation is now an imperative in preparation for the mission of all, including religious. It has seen a shift in response to the displacement and movement of people but also in response to clergy and religious from former mission countries coming to minister in Western

---

[10] *Starting Afresh from Christ*, 3, 9, 10.
[11] *Starting Afresh from Christ*, 34, 37–45.

countries. Notwithstanding these developments in the under-standing of mission, the primary meaning of mission remains sending: sending by God to share in His mission. However, the mission is single: it is God's mission. There are not as many missions as there are religious congregations.

Within religious congregations lack of conceptual clarity on the single mission is at the root of the loss of energy which many religious congregations experience some time after their general chapters have taken place. This is more than a natural wilting of enthusiasm and energy associated with a pivotal event in the life of the congregation. It seems to me that many chapters have failed to understand the nature of the task before them and have expended great effort in producing chapter mission statements to which scant attention is paid by the members in the years between one chapter and the next.[12] Congregations then set up committees or task groups in order to establish why it was that the energy of the chapter dissipated and had not been dis-seminated throughout the congregation. Lack of energy for dissemination and implementation is related less to the levels of participation in chapter and more to the failure to appreciate the true task of chapter. In other words, religious set themselves up for the dilution of energy in the post-chapter period because chapters have not asked the right question of themselves or appreciated their true function.

I suggest further that the preoccupation with rewriting mission may be partly attributed to the elevation of charism to the status of mission or to the conflation of the terms. Without *missio Dei*, there would be no charism: the whole notion is redundant. Therefore charism derives from mission and the charism of religious orders is about the shaping of the single mission for particular groups and distinct historical and cultural circumstances but charism does not constitute the mission.

In this regard, leaders have a particular responsibility to inform, and form, chapter facilitators. Given the importance of the general chapter in the life of congregations, I suggest leaders

---

[12] Elizabeth M. Cotter, *The General Chapter in a Religious Institute with Particular Reference to the IBVM Loreto Branch* (Bern: Peter Lang, n.d).

and pre-chapter committees would do well to attend to the selection of facilitators with great care and, in their pre-engagement conversations with them, devote less time to the operations and logistics of chapters and more time to arriving at a shared understanding of the chapter's true purpose. Another responsibility of leaders in this regard is to act responsibly. Timothy Radcliffe deftly describes the cycle of irresponsibility that beleaguers difficult questions. All too often such questions are passed up several levels of authority, end up in a chapter commission which may take some years to produce a consultation paper, and then spiral downwards through the very same levels through which they ascended, only to be held in reserve for the next general chapter. Stagnation and paralysis in decision-making related to chapters is another pernicious element in the prevention of implementation.[13]

The most recent examination by the church of the context for mission is to be found in the Synod of Bishops, XIII Ordinary General Assembly, 'The New Evangelisation for the Transmission of the Christian Faith', which took place from the 7–28 October 2012. New Evangelisation is concerned with a fresh proclamation of Christ in a rapidly changing world and for this an understanding of the new and emerging context was essential. '[The] situation is requiring the church to consider in an entirely new way how she proclaims and transmits the faith,' asserted one of the preparatory documents, continuing that the task requires a bold approach, 'it is the courage to forge new paths in responding to the changing circumstances'. Along with new paths, 'new tools and new expressions' were necessary to enable the 'word of faith be heard more and be better understood … even in the new deserts of this world'.[14] The preparatory documents, the *Lineamenta* and the *Instrumentum Laboris (IL)*, published in January and July 2012 respectively, along with the synodal

---

[13] Timothy Radcliffe, *Sing a New Song: The Christian Vocation* (Dublin: Dominican Publications, 1999), p. 37.

[14] Synod of Bishops, XIII Ordinary General Assembly of Bishops, The New Evangelization for the Transmission of the Christian Faith, *Lineamenta* (January, 2012), 3, 5; *Instrumentum Laboris* (July 2012), 8.

documents, the *Relatio Post Disceptionem (RPD)*, the propositions and the Message to the People of God, all published in October 2012, may be seen as the most recent statements of the church's thinking on the context of mission in the twenty-first century.[15]

The church seeks to understand the world in which the new evangelisation will be applied and, in the *Lineamenta* chapter, 'Time for a New Evangelisation', six sectors calling for new evangelisation are nominated: cultural; social; social communication; economic; scientific and technological research; civic and political. In the elaboration of these sectors of the contemporary context of society, there are few surprises. Secularisation is the dominant theme of the cultural sector while migration and globalisation are the principal themes of the social sector.[16] Secularisation is characterised by the attempt to engage in life without reference to the Transcendent. In the *IL* it is further characterised as a subdued secularism, that is to say not hostile, but indifferent, and thus a more insidious interloper in the life of the Christian. The *IL* rescues itself from total subscription to a subtraction theory by reference to the positive lessons Christianity has imbibed from secularisation and the possibility of engagement between believers and non-believers.[17] The widespread effects of secularisation amongst all cultures is briefly acknowledged in the *Relatio Post Disceptionem* (*RPD*) and secularism and indifference are joined in the interventions of

---

[15] Synod of Bishops, XIII Ordinary General Assembly of Bishops, The New Evangelization for the Transmission of the Christian Faith, *Relatio Post Disceptationem*, Bulletin 21, 17 October 2012; Final List of Propositions, Bulletin 33, 27 October 2012; Message to the People of God concluding the 13th XIII Ordinary General Assembly of Bishops 7–28 October 2012. At the time of writing the Post-Synodal Apostolic Exhortation has not been published.

[16] The responses to the *Lineamenta* of *Vita Consecrata* identified a wide range of negative contextual impacts: indifference, secularism, hedonism, consumerism, individualism, rejection of authority.

[17] Indifference rather than opposition or declared neutrality is a feature of the post-secular state, see discussion in Dermot A. Lane, *Stepping Stones to Other Religious: A Christian Theology of Inter-religious Dialogue* (Dublin: Veritas, 2011), pp. 3–34; *IL*, 54.

many of the bishops. Secularisation is the specific subject of Proposition 8: Witnessing in a Secularised World. Contemporary Christians, it avers, are like the first Christians but there is both challenge and possibility. The scriptural metaphors of little flock, salt of the earth, light to the world are evoked to inspire the faithful to greater and more faithful witness. Nevertheless it can be argued that Proposition 8 retreats partially from the possibility of engagement offered in the *RPD* and constitutes a lost opportunity to participate in shaping the contextual features of our society and engage with the other actors in the process.

The great migration of peoples is unequivocally discussed in terms of loss to the individuals who migrate and erosion of their bonds of community, cultural and religious identity. The *IL* links secularisation with migration, resulting in a combination which adds to the diffusion and dilution of the elements of religious cultures. This point is reiterated in the *RPD* while the measures proposed in Proposition 21 in support of migrants are antidotes to the losses described earlier. Although migration has its darker side as itemised in the Proposition, nowhere is there an expression of the depth of faith and the richness of its expression which many migrants bring from their countries of origin to their new countries.

Undoubtedly as religious live in the world, they, and the structures they populate, are subject to the same influences of secularisation as are all other persons and institutions. One contextual factor which has a serious impact on religious life, and is of concern to many leaders, is the sense of individualism which is a by-product of secularisation. When coupled with a mistaken understanding of discernment, then all ministry becomes a matter of individual predilection or choice and availability for mission is subordinated to personal preference. Discernment becomes a process whereby the individual considers the advantages and disadvantages to her of what has been proposed, may consult a spiritual director and then reports her decision to leadership. Leaders are excluded from the discernment process and become the mere recipients of the outcome of discernment rather than discernment partners. The sense of entrenchment is very difficult for leaders to break and can impede, or strangle, efforts for implementation of the *missio Dei* according to the charism of particular congregations. This point is noted in *Starting Afresh from Christ* when referring to the lights and shadows of consecrated life today, 'the prevalence of personal projects over community endeavours can deeply corrode the communion of brotherly and sisterly love'.[18]

One factor underlying this sense of entrenchment and resulting unavailability for mission lies in an ambivalent, and occasionally hostile, attitude to obedience which, in most cases, is based on an immature understanding of obedience and its relationship to freedom. Obedience is particularly difficult for those who do not yet realise, in the words of *Vita Consecrata*, that 'there is no contradiction between obedience and freedom'.[19] Leaders need to be both patient and unwavering in their efforts to bring about a greater understanding of the freedom of obedience.

Two other contextual features, women and child sexual abuse, require some attention before we move to the loci of mission for religious in the contemporary world. Both *Vita Consecrata* and *Starting Afresh from Christ* had strongly affirmed the place of women religious in the church's mission. The new self-awareness of women is credited with challenging and changing the perspectives of men and *Vita Consecrata* goes so far as to say that the future of evangelisation is unimaginable without women, and especially, consecrated women.[20] Both documents assert that, as a matter of urgency, the way must be opened for the participation of women religious 'in different fields and at all levels including decision-making processes'.[21] This sense of urgency is absent from the synodal documents which do not break any new ground. Proposition 46: Collaboration of Men and Women in the Church, claims that pastors have recognised the special nurturing and compassionate capacities of women expressed especially in their role as mothers. The Proposition acknowledges situations it

---

[18] *Starting Afresh from Christ*, 12.
[19] *Vita Consecrata*, 96.
[20] Ibid., 57.
[21] Ibid., 58; *Starting Afresh from Christ*, 9.

claims exist: that women, lay and religious, contribute with men to theological reflection at all levels and that they share pastoral responsibilities in new ways. Sadly, whatever gains were made in the inclusion and appointment of women, and women religious, to roles of influence and decision-making in mission, and there were many, are in grave danger of being eroded by a new conservatism more obvious in some seminarians and recently ordained priests than in some members of the episcopacy. The reduction of the role of women appears as a badge of orthodoxy among some new young conservatives. In the same vein, a careful initiation into the role of women in the church and women religious is a vital component of inculturation programmes for priests from former mission areas who come to serve in Western countries.

The church proclaims herself to be a listening church, 'a hearer and disciple' but nowhere in the *Lineamenta* for the Synod on New Evangelisation is there the faintest acknowledgement of the existence of child sexual abuse nor an appreciation of its impact on the world in which religious seek to carry out the mission of God. Unbelievably, the term 'abuse' is reserved for terrorism.[22] Sexual abuse has devastating consequences for the abused but also pain for those of our brothers in religious life and secular priesthood who lead lives of dedicated service and fidelity to the vows and promises they made. The *IL* for the same synod appears to take a very tentative step in acknowledging abuse when speaking of the sinfulness of the church's members and counter witness given by infidelity to one's vocation. If these are truly references to abuse then they are so opaque as to be embarrassing, and if they are not, then there is a mystifying silence. Moreover, the reference to infidelity comes in a subordinate clause where the main clause urges us not to 'underestimate the *mysterium iniquitatis* which the Dragon waged on the rest of the offspring of the Woman'.[23] Is this the language of 'new tools and approaches' which speaks to people of the twenty-first century? More importantly, the failure to admit unequivocally in a study of the

---

[22] New Evangelization, *Lineamenta*, 2, 6.
[23] Ibid., *Instrumentum Laboris*, 35.

contemporary context that abuse exists and that it has deeply eroded trust in the clergy and hierarchy was too much of the old and not nearly enough of the new in the preparations for a synod on the new evangelisation. The Synod itself did not equivocate. Proposition 49: Pastoral Dimension of the Ordained Ministry, naming priests as the primary agents of the new evangelisation, a statement with which some might disagree, goes on to speak of 'the scandals affecting priestly life and ministry, which we deeply regret'. At least here the language is unambiguous and removed from the euphemisms of the synodal preparatory documents.

The role of religious in the new evangelisation is muted in the *Lineamenta*. Mentioned after the new ecclesial movements, it is stated that the consecrated life has a great role to play in the new evangelisation. Consecrated persons are included in a list of groups, gathered around the bishop, who will have a part to play in the new evangelisation in the local churches but they are excluded from the list of those who 'have long been engaged in the work of evangelisation and education (bishops, priests, catechists, educators, teachers, and parents)'.[24] It seems a long way from *Vita Consecrata*'s clarion call that evangelisation was unthinkable without the contribution of religious. *Starting Afresh from Christ* offered a richer treatment of the place of religious in the mission of the church. One finds appreciation and admiration for the contribution of religious in traditional spheres of activity and in new ministries. The document singles out those religious who 'push the Gospel forward to the border' in their service to the excluded, in particular, displaced persons and migrants.[25]

However the responses summarised in the Synod *IL* convey quite a strong sense of the role of apostolic religious through a statement of appreciation of the importance of religious life, hope for its continued cultural contribution in education, health, pastoral service and orientation of the activity of religious to the materially and spiritually poor.[26] It is as if the hierarchy had to be reminded of religious by the local churches. The propositions are more positive than the preparatory documents. Proposition 50

---

[24] Ibid., *Lineamenta*, 8, 17, 20.

[25] *Starting Afresh from Christ*, 9.

[26] New Evangelization, *Instrumentum Laboris*, 114.

affirms the role of religious in the new evangelisation, calls for a radical, joyful witness and, echoing *Starting Afresh from Christ* quoted above, asks religious to be ready to go to the 'geographical, social and cultural frontiers of evangelization'. Religious are to be active in grasping the opportunities presented by secularism to engage with others at various points along the continuum of secularisation and faith in God.

Responses to the Synod *Lineamenta* called for a whole-church approach to priestly vocations and the *IL* calls on priests and clerical religious to attend to their lifestyle so that they give witness to the attraction of their vocation. The same applies to those in consecrated life, especially institutes for women.[27] One can detect here a sense of the golden-age mentality. Doubtless vocation recruitment is an issue, and in other contexts, doctrinal error has to be corrected, perhaps some pastoral directions need to be reoriented, but there can be no going back, a point well made by Gregory Collins in his contribution to *A Future Full of Hope?*[28] Hankering after a golden age bathed in nostalgia will not generate energy for the *missio Dei* nor respond to the needs of those who are waiting patiently at the edge. In this sense the synodal documents fall short. They give no hint of an incisive analysis of the context of today's society. The *RPD* and propositions do not fully liberate themselves from the narrow approach of the preparatory documents nor challenge the shaping of the Synod by them. There is little that is new in the discussion of the new evangelisation and little that religious can take with them in refining their charism for the sake of the mission of God.

The Second Vatican Council told us that we must read the signs of the times. At least twenty years before he was elected Abbot of Glenstal, Mark Patrick Hederman wrote *The Haunted Inkwell: Art and Our Future*. Hederman envisages the construction of the future as the work of artists. He accords the task of reading

[27] Ibid., 84.
[28] Gregory Collins, 'Giving Religious Life a Theology Transfusion', in Gemma Simmonds, ed., *A Future Full of Hope?* (Dublin: Columba, 2012), pp. 23–37.

the signs of the times not to social commentators, economists, politicians, or episcopal synods but to poets. In respect of Seamus Heaney's poem 'Glanmore Revisited', Hederman writes that the poet is one who 'stares, squints, angles, aims and peeps through doors, half-doors, thresholds, awnings, openings, sky lights and windows'.[29] The poet is then a seer of possibilities, not of cemented certainties. 'The Skylight', the seventh sonnet of 'Glanmore Revisited', describes the house the poet wants to reconstruct on his return to Glanmore. He did not want to cut into the roof to make a skylight as the unidentified 'you' of the poem did. The slates kept in the heat but, 'when the slates came off, extravagant Sky entered and held surprise wide open'.[30] This is a compelling metaphor for religious life and mission: God's love, extravagant Sky, holds surprise wide open and invites us to move into the space.

How are we to choreograph this space, how are we to speak in it or are we to speak at all? It is cautionary to recall the message of José Comblin, which goes beyond vocabulary, in his now more than 30-year-old work *The Meaning of Mission* where he writes,

> there is a real danger that the church may end up talking so much to its own members that it will forget that its mission is to go out and speak to other human beings. It may end up talking and listening to itself, so that its mission and the church itself really disappear.[31]

The processes of the *Lineamenta* and the *Instrumentum Laboris* are limited: from the centre to the inner circle of local churches. Do the wider circles of other churches, of other religions, of humanist societies, of artists and poets have nothing to say that might be useful to the church's discernment of the signs of the times? In the poem 'A Prayer for Old Age', William Butler Yeats told us to think with the whole of our being:

---

[29] Mark Patrick Hederman, *The Haunted Inkwell: Art and our Future* (Dublin, Columba Press, 2001), p. 182.

[30] Seamus Heaney, 'Glanmire Revisited', *Seeing Things*, (London: Faber and Faber, 1991), p. 37.

[31] José Comblin, *The Meaning of Mission: Jesus Christians and the Wayfaring Church*, trans. John Drury (Dublin: Gill and Macmillan, 1979), p. 34.

> God guard me from those thoughts men think
> In the mind alone;
> He that sings a lasting song
> Thinks in a marrow-bone.

Might not the church benefit from an engagement with the marrow-bone of the wider society in its consideration of what it is useful to discuss in a synod on evangelisation? The presence at the Synod of Archbishop Rowan Williams and the Ecumenical Patriarch, Bartholomew I, is to be welcomed but surely is not enough to remove the slates and let Extravagant Sky shine through.

For many years in the last century, one could scarcely come across the term religious life without the adjective 'prophetic' applied to it. But what does it mean? It has been suggested that the inclination of religious to dub their lives prophetic may well be a compensation for loss of identity.[32] In the context of prophetic leadership I call to mind a twenty-first-century prophet named Ted Kennedy, a priest of the Archdiocese of Sydney who died in 2005. Ted was the parish priest of Redfern, an inner-city suburb of Sydney and home to many Australian Aborigines from several tribes of New South Wales. Poor health, poor housing, alcohol, and drugs made Redfern an undesirable place in the eyes of many non-Aboriginal people. Ted ministered there for over thirty years. The tribute paid to Ted in the State Parliament of NSW by the then Deputy Premier and Minister for Aboriginal Affairs, Dr Andrew Refshauge, identifies some of the qualities of a contemporary prophet,

> Ted Kennedy's conscience was a goad to the mighty and a balm to the needy. It led him to where, before him, many would not go ... It made him beloved. It made him contentious. It put him at odds with the police. It stirred him to anger and mercy, sorrow and great forgiveness, and long nights of the soul. It was said of Ted at his funeral that he was a holy man, a living treasure, a pebble in the comfortable boot of the establishment, an untidy

---

[32] Radcliffe, *Sing a New Song*, p. 210; Letourneau, 'Responses to the *Lineamenta*', 9.

prophet and an enemy of cruel blindness and petty pomp who ended his life with empty pockets and dirty hands, his life poured out for all.[33]

Here indeed are some of the elements of prophetic religious life but Ted himself was a quiet man, no writer of speeches or maker of manifestos. His prophetic voice was heard among his people, those in his pastoral charge and those he encountered in pursuit of his mission: pastor to the people of Redfern, face of Christ to the Aboriginal people. Ted's example shows that a prophetic stance does not require the taking on of greatly politicised positions or causes, though these may be necessary at times, but is recognised in devotion to the poor and those in our care. Similar confirmation was evident at the outbreak of the Leadership Conference of Women Religious issue, the public perception equating a prophetic stance with visibility in the service of the poor in traditional and new ministries, along with the personal sacrifice made by religious in pursuit of the mission.[34] The tendency to locate the prophetic role of religious solely at the edge is limited in its understanding of the prophetic role itself and can be dismissive of religious and the hierarchy whose ministry is not at the edge but who are united in mission with those who are.[35]

The prophetic dimension of religious life still resides in the more traditional loci of the ministry of religious: hospitals; schools; refuges; disadvantaged youth; migrants; refugees; women in distress and more. Yet some religious have been shaken and dispirited by the idea that such service is no longer one in which religious should be engaged because other, lay, people are

---

[33] 'NSW Legislative Assembly Hansard and Papers, Thursday 26 May 2005', *Parliament of New South Wales* [website] <http://www.parliament.nsw.gov.au/prod/web/common.nsf/V3HH BHome> accessed 12 September 2012.

[34] Reference here is to the Vatican's much-publicised quarrel with the Leadership Conference of Women Religious in the United States of America.

[35] Letourneau, 'Responses to the *Lineamenta*', 12.

now equipped for such service. Repeated so often that it has almost assumed the status of dogma, is the idea that the church acts in welfare or social services only where the state does not, or cannot, act. To put it the other way round: if the state is sufficiently engaged in social service, then the church does not need to be. *Deus Caritas Est* states unequivocally that the 'church's deepest nature is expressed in her threefold responsibility of proclaiming the Word of God, celebrating the sacraments, and exercising the ministry of charity'.[36] Charity, the works of love, is part of the nature of the church, of her essence. It follows then that no matter how munificent the state may be, or how effective its delivery of service, the church cannot opt out of works of love because she cannot deny her own nature. Therefore the church must always be involved in works of love. We engage in ministry because the love of God calls us to mission and not because governments aren't doing an adequate job,

> There is no ordering of the State so just that it can eliminate the need for a service of love.[37]

The idea that any society could be so justly ordered that it would render works of love superfluous rests on a purely materialist concept of the human person, the idea that 'man can live by bread alone'.

In service to the poor and social justice advocacy, religious are the face of Christ and of the church. We can be, and indeed are, present in places where the official church is absent: and thus we are in a privileged place. Religious live in the revolving door of the church, figuratively speaking. We meet people on their path into and on their way from the church. Through the ministry of religious, many people encounter Christ before they encounter him in a parish Eucharistic community. It is with religious that many share their disappointments with the church and their sadness in being estranged from it.

Since the Second Vatican Council there have been great changes in aspects of religious life. At first, and especially for

---

[36] Benedict XVI, *Deus Caritas Est*, 25 December 2005, 25 (a).
[37] *Deus Caritas Est*, 28 (b).

women's congregations, the most visible change was the habit, then new areas of ministry in response to fresh understanding of the charism and new needs in society, for example, HIV/AIDS, and varied arrangements for community life. Mission, perhaps, was the least contentious of all topics but I suggest today that, paradoxically, it is in the understanding of mission that much of the tension within religious life, and between religious congregations and the hierarchy lies. All God's people share in the one mission of God. The church and religious congregations are servants of the one mission. In this common servanthood lies the first and fundamental point of tension.

One model of religious life in the church sees the centre occupied by the bureaucratic organs of the church and the edge populated by the poor and marginalised with whom religious are to be found. This view is well established and recently articulated by Martha Zechmeister in a stimulating address to the 2012 Annual Conference of Religious of Ireland (CORI).[38] Mission is exercised in the church along trajectories from the centre outwards and from the liminal spaces inwards. When the trajectories intersect there can be tension (and the odd collision) but if they were never to meet, danger would loom. Tension, in this context, is healthy; it is a sign of life rather than a confirmation of stagnation.

As noted above, the responses to the *Lineamenta* for *Vita Consecrata* raised the matter of strained relationships within the church, suggesting that women religious were struggling to find their place within it. In their view the hierarchy did not evince a sympathetic understanding of religious life for women and seemed to show some preference for the emerging ecclesial movements.[39] *Vita Consecrata* and *Starting Afresh from Christ* responded from the foundations of *Lumen Gentium* that consecrated life is one of the essential elements of the church. In *Vita Consecrata*, religious are to feel with the church, *sentire cum*

---

[38] Martha Zechmeister CJ, 'Passion for God, Compassion for the Other', *Religious Life Review*, 51:276, September/
October 2012, pp. 261–74.
[39] Letourneau, 'Overview of Responses', 12.

ecclesia; they are called to be experts in communion but in *Starting Afresh from Christ* 'experts in communion' is sharpened to

> it is impossible to contemplate the face of God without seeing it shine in that of the church. To love Christ is to love the church in her persons and institutions.[40]

The language has been turned around to read that anyone who loves the church cannot criticise her. In *Vita Consecrata* allegiance of mind and heart for the magisterium of the bishops is claimed as a distinctive element of such communion. *Starting Afresh from Christ* maintains the same line but turns it into a loyalty test, 'proof of unity', rather than an expression of communion.[41] In plain fact, both documents require allegiance to the magisterium but the change in vocabulary and tone in the latter is more than stylistic. *Vita Consecrata* offered reassurance on the point about the new ecclesial communities, affirming the 'pre-eminent' place accorded to existing institutions, an endorsement repeated in *Starting Afresh from Christ*.[42]

Although the strong continuity between the documents and the nuances of difference are noted, it is arguable that the religious who raised these concerns in the first place would not have been satisfied with the responses because the matters they raised were not material for the magisterium but related more to how authority is exercised rather than who has the ultimate authority. There was, however, one leap forward in this memorable statement from *Vita Consecrata* about dialogue, 'Dialogue is the new name of charity especially charity within the church.'[43]

Without advancing a view on the doctrinal substance of the interaction between the Congregation for the Doctrine of the Faith (CDF) and the Leadership Conference of Women Religious (LCWR), one can see in this interaction a clear illustration of the tension to which I refer. Bearing in mind that the core business of

---

[40] *Vita Consecrata*, 29, 46; *Starting Afresh from Christ*, 32.

[41] *Vita Consecrata*, 46; *Starting Afresh from Christ*, 32.

[42] *Vita Consecrata*, 62, quoted also in *Starting Afresh from Christ*, 30.

[43] *Vita Consecrata*, 74.

newspapers is to sell newspapers and therefore highlight the conflictual elements of any issue, the tide of editorial opinion and popular opinion in Los Angeles at the time of the CDF's intervention, favoured 'the nuns', as Cardinal Timothy Dolan blogged, 'we Catholics love the nuns, Americans love the nuns,' and later in the same blog, 'Rome loves the sisters.'[44] Cardinal O'Malley had earlier called the whole business a public relations debacle apparently without realising that his comment exacerbated the issue by relegating the debate to a message which had to be managed, thereby reinforcing the view that religious women were a problem rather than a partnership rich in potential for the mission of the church.[45]

The immediate past president of the LCWR, Sr Pat Farrell, averred that the 'inherent existential tension between the complementary roles of hierarchy and religious is not likely to change'.[46] In reading her text, it is difficult to know if she wished that it would change. But it does not have to change. The inherent tension is a factor which affects any group in the church when, in a shared mission, the actors do not share equality of authority. It is not necessarily a criticism to point to the existence of the phenomenon. Whether conscious at the time of *Vita Consecrata*'s statement that 'Dialogue is the new name of charity especially charity within the church', the LCWR determined that the path of dialogue was the way forward. The 2012 assembly of LCWR 'charged the board to conduct their conversation with Archbishop Sartain from a stance of mutual respect, careful listening and open dialogue' and the board's brief report on its meeting with the archbishop again emphasised the mutuality of dialogue referring

[44] Cardinal Timothy Dolan, *The Gospel in the Digital Age* [Blog] <http://blog.archny.org> accessed 11 September 2012.
[45] Quoted in Joshua McElwee, 'LCWR: Vatican meeting "difficult" with "differing perspectives"', *National Catholic Reporter* [website], 18 June 2012. <http://ncronline.org/blogs/ncr-today/lcwr-vatican-meeting-%C3%ABdifficult-differing-perspectives> accessed 11 September 2012.
[46] Pat Farrell OSF, '"Navigating the Shifts", Presidential Address, LCWR Assembly 2012', *LCWR* [website], 10 August 2012. <https://lcwr.org/media/news/navigating-shifts-presidential-address-pat-farrell-osf> accessed 9 September 2012.

to openness and honesty on their part and the Archbishop's careful listening and request to learn more about the Conference and the members' views on religious life.[47] Some may choose to interpret the language as aspirational, and overly irenic, but the path towards resolution is a true test of commitment to dialogue which is distinct from a commitment to compromise.

Notwithstanding the affirmations cited in the documents above, and mindful of the point on strained relations between religious and the hierarchy enunciated in the *Lineamenta* for *Vita Consecrata*, one is justified in asking if there is not some loss of confidence in religious on the part of the church hierarchy. In my view, this sense leaches from the pages of official documents from time to time. Consider the recommendation addressed to religious for implementing the Year of Faith,

> During this time, members of Institutes of Consecrated Life and of Societies of Apostolic Life are asked to work towards the new evangelization with a renewed union to the Lord Jesus, each according to their proper charism, in fidelity to the Holy Father and to sound doctrine.[48]

The recommendation is underwhelming, unimaginative, and, in truth, not specific to religious. It seems tired and pedestrian: gone are the vim, verve and drive associated with the prophetic dimension of religious life.

It is apparent to me that some religious understand the charism-driven mission of their religious congregation to be completely separate from the mission of God in the church. I have no way of knowing if this conviction has grown since *Vita Consecrata* but it certainly has not disappeared. The *IL* for the Synod on the New Evangelisation reveals that there were calls to discuss the 'relationship between charism and institution,

---

[47] 'LCWR Statement on Meeting with Archbishop Sartain', *LCWR* [website], 13 August 2012 <https://lcwr.org/media/lcwr-statement-meeting-archbishop-sartain>

[48] Congregation for the Doctrine of the Faith, *Note with Pastoral Recommendations for the Year of Faith*, 2012, IV, 7.

charismatic gifts and hierarchical gifts' and talk of '"co-essentiality"of these gifts of the Spirit, in the life and mission of the Church'.[49] This promising approach is due no doubt to some vigorous and robust responses which lurk beneath the measured prose of the *Instrumentum Laboris* which itself adds colour and new tones to the paler palette of the *Lineamenta*. The relationship between hierarchical and charismatic gifts is recommended for further study at diocesan and inter-diocesan level by Proposition 43 of the Synod which affirms co-essentiality over competition but within a hierarchical framework. The affirmation confirms that the basis of tension lies in the phenomenon of common servanthood exercised by groups with different authority in the church.

Some religious have responded to this tension by trying to ignore what they term as the institutional church and it is incumbent on them to refine their sensitivities to the ecclesial ground of *missio Dei*. Conversely, some members of the hierarchy need to re-envision religious not as a group carrying out one of many works of the diocese but as consecrated persons and members of institutes in collaboration with them in the *missio Dei*. Leaders in religious congregations are responsible for holding both the ecclesial dimension of religious life before their members and holding the ground for the exercise of the particular charism of their respective institutes.

Structures do not operate independently of people. There are innumerable cases of fruitful and harmonious cooperation between clergy/bishops and religious in many pastoral settings. Of course there are truly dedicated religious, with a mature understanding of their mission in the church, religious who are able to forge great partnerships with clergy and laity and who joyfully witness to the love of God in their lives. So we need not despair but listen again to the beautifully worked passage from Mark's Gospel which recounts the healing of the blind beggar, Bartimaeus (Mark 10: 46–52). The passage is well known for its moving and eloquent depiction of the mercy and compassion of

---

[49] New Evangelization, *Instrumentum Laboris*, 116.

Jesus, but I draw your attention to the disciples of Jesus and to the words Mark gives them. When Jesus stopped and told the disciples to call Bartimaeus to him, they said to the beggar, 'Courage ... get up, he is calling you.' That is how I finish today, Courage – get up, he is calling us!

Reflection Questions

1. 'Our mission consists essentially not in what we do but in being sent to extend God's reign in creation and in the world.' What do you understand by this? Do you agree?

2. The author speaks of the difficulty some congregations have in turning their chapter documents into reality. Why do you think this happens? What could be done to remedy this?

3. The author speaks of 'the sense of individualism which is a by-product of secularisation' and its effect on mission. What do you understand by this? What significance does it have for community life, mission and the living or the vows?

5

The Challenge of Community Today

Patricia Rumsey PC

In this chapter, I will begin by setting out the ideal *Perfectae Caritatis* gives us of community according to Vatican II's vision of 'renewed and adapted' religious life and then discuss the validity and practicality of this understanding of community today, fifty years on. Vatican II presented the religious community as the place where religious live out their personal commitment to God expressed in the three traditional vows of poverty, chastity and obedience, hopefully in a way that enables them to grow and mature as people. However, the secular world in which we live and the world of religious life have both changed almost unrecognisably in the past fifty years, and so I will look at some of the problems of applying this ideal in today's world. *Perfectae Caritatis* tells us,

> Common life, in prayer and the sharing of the same spirit (Acts 2:42), should be constant, after the example of the early Church, in which the company of believers were of one heart and soul. It should be nourished by the teaching of the Gospel and by the sacred liturgy, especially by the Eucharist. Religious, as members of Christ, should live together as brothers and should give pride of place to one another in esteem (cf. Rom. 12:10), carrying one another's burdens (cf. Gal. 6:12).[1]

Perfectae Caritatis sets a high ideal before us, but while upholding the ideal I question the foundations on which it is built. The purpose of *Perfectae Caritatis* was 'The Appropriate

---

[1] Austin Flannery, ed., 'Decree On the Up-to-Date Renewal of Religious Life', *Perfectae Caritatis (1965), Second Ecumenical Council of the Vatican* (Dublin: Dominican Publications, 1975), p. 15.

Renewal and Adaptation of Religious Life' and states that this will be brought about by a return to the sources.[2] However, in this context, reform is usually understood as looking backwards from a present which is perceived as being less-than-perfect to a past golden age where everything was faultless, in order to recreate this supposed ideal time in the present.[3] An especially good example of this tendency is presented in the Acts of the Apostles. Within religious life, reform has frequently been interpreted as an attempt to return to the 'pure' Christianity presented by Luke in Acts.[4] However, there is currently less certainty about Luke's account of the early church. It is thought rather to reflect the idealistic view held by the second generation of Christians about their beginnings and to suggest a situation which may not actually have existed in reality in the earliest community.[5] This image created in Acts is at once idealistic and theoretical, and it is thought that the practical reality of life in the early church is to be seen in other early Christian writings such as the *Didache*.[6] It is now thought that Acts looks back with longing to the perceived halcyon days of early Christianity and portrays them according to this idealised vision.[7] *Perfectae Caritatis* rightly encourages us to look back to our founders:

---

[2] *Perfectae Caritatis*, 2 (b).

[3] See Mircea Eliade, *The Myth of the Eternal Return* (Princeton: Princeton University Press, 1971).

[4] See Gerhart Ladner, *The Idea of Reform* (Cambridge, MA: Harvard University Press, 1959), pp. 341–7.

[5] G. S. Wakefield, *An Outline of Christian Worship* (Edinburgh: T & T Clark, 1998), p. 10. See also Bruce Chilton, *Redeeming Time: the Wisdom of Ancient Jewish and Christian Festal Calendars* (Peabody, MA: Hendrickson, 2002), p. 73.

[6] See Thomas O'Loughlin, 'The Didache as a Source for Picturing the Earliest Christian Communities: The Case of the Practice of Fasting', in K. O'Mahony, ed., *Christian Origins: Worship, Belief and Society* (Sheffield: Sheffield Academic Press, 2003), pp. 83–112.

[7] Even the text of Acts as we now have it portrays a less-than-ideal church, where there was plenty of all-too-human bickering and disagreement; see Acts 6:1; 11:1–3; 15:1–2; 15:36–40. There are also many passages in Paul's letters which display a less-than-perfect church.

The up-to-date renewal of the religious life comprises both a constant return to the sources of the whole of the Christian life and to the primitive inspiration of the institutes. ... Therefore the spirit and aims of each founder should be faithfully accepted and retained.[8]

However, this has to be done with circumspection; Ladner's work on the myth of reform demonstrates that this desire to look back and see a perfect past either in the earliest Christian community or in the early days of our own orders or congregations, is, in reality, a reflection of the idealistic longings of the current generation and this is an issue of which we have to beware in our efforts to 'renew and adapt', otherwise our expectations will be unreal and will be doomed to disappointment. Religious today are struggling in and with situations very different from those which existed in the mid to late sixties and which Vatican II certainly had not foreseen and the theology of religious life now presents a very different face. We can compare these situations from the sixties with current life and thought by looking at the section on religious life in *Lumen Gentium* when the differences will become very clear:

Members of these (religious) families ... have a stable and more solidly based way of Christian life. They receive well-proven teaching on seeking after perfection. They are bound together in brotherly communion in the army of Christ. Their Christian freedom is fortified by obedience. Thus they are enabled to live securely and to maintain faithfully the religious life to which they have pledged themselves.[9]

This probably described fairly accurately, if somewhat idealistically, the situation in religious houses in the sixties; but very few religious today feel that their communities are experiencing a 'stable and solidly based' way of life. In the present climate for many, if not most, religious the future is insecure and uncertain, the survival of their way of life is in doubt, and the years since Vatican II have been a painful journey.

---

[8] *Perfectae Caritatis*, 2 (b).
[9] *Lumen Gentium*, 43.

They have seen their houses close, sisters leave, their congregations amalgamate, their numbers dwindle, the apostolic work to which they had dedicated their lives be handed over to others. Their life has been anything but 'stable and secure'. Religious jargon, too, has changed. No religious today would describe the religious life as 'seeking after perfection' and although the teaching of our respective founders can be said to be 'well-founded' as they all based this teaching on the gospel, it has to be transposed and lived out in a very different world from that in which it was first written, often many centuries ago. Military figures of speech such as 'the army of Christ' would not be phrases of choice to describe religious life today, and, of course, no one would today speak of 'brothers' without adding 'sisters'. These anomalies and anachronisms, even in one of the most far reaching of the documents of Vatican II, the one which proclaimed the 'universal call to holiness', show how much the world of religious life has changed in the last fifty years. In recent decades there has been real progress in our understanding of human dignity which has brought, in its wake, an awareness of the equality of rights between women and men. The Universal Declaration of Human Rights has been both the fruit of, and brought about by, a revolution in our attitude to the human person. The place of women, at least in the Western world, has changed out of all recognition from the world our mothers knew. Our understanding of and our attitude towards authority, and consequently our concept of obedience, has evolved mightily. Leadership in religious congregations and communities is now seen in the form of service rather than that of authority. Information technology has revolutionised the way we communicate. All these factors have changed our understanding and our living out of religious life in community so that today we are still motivated by the ideals of Vatican II, but we are trying to live them out in a very different world.

Sandra Schneiders writes of 'the extreme rigidity and uniformity of religious life in the post-Tridentine period' and I think those of us who were around before 1965 can bear witness to the fact that before Vatican II, conformity was, by and large, the name of the game.[10] 'Maintaining faithfully the religious life to which we have pledged ourselves' was usually achieved by institutionalisation: strong internal and external structures, definite and frequently all-but-impermeable boundaries between religious life and what was referred to as 'the world' and the 'time-honoured traditions' and customs of which *Perfectae Caritatis* speaks. When these structures, boundaries and customs were either deliberately removed, thankfully collapsed or simply died the death, many religious, not having internalised the values they were ideally supposed to enshrine, were unable to cope and, in weariness or disillusionment, gave up the battle, and turned their backs on a way of life which, for whatever reason, no longer had meaning for them. In the aftermath of Vatican II, some (and this was not necessarily the more elderly among our number) took refuge in a return-to-the-past mentality, where security was to be found in a somewhat legalistic mentality of 'keeping the rules' which had worked, apparently, for previous generations. Others of us took up the challenge of 'renewal and adaptation', returned to the sources, which for some meant encountering those sources for the first time, and, as a fruit of this new understanding, tried to put the spirit and charism of our founders to work actively in the present day world, a world very different from that in which our rules had originally been written. Though feeling at times battered and bruised at the criticism from many sources which became our lot, and the lack of support and understanding we sometimes experienced even from the institutional church, and the fewness of new recruits to take up the torch for future generations, we have soldiered on.

This, although describing the present reality for many individuals and communities, all sounds very negative; the questions remain: on the positive front, what do we have to offer future generations? What have we learned from the pain of past years about living religious life in community? What positive

---

[10] Sandra Schneiders, 'The Changing Shape and Function of Community Life', in *New Wineskins: Re-imagining Religious Life Today* (New York: Paulist Press, 1986), pp. 236–65.

conclusions can we draw from what have sometimes been negative experiences? Can we show the world the joy and fulfilment of a life lived for Christ together with others who share our commitment and our ideals, even in today's somewhat straightened circumstances when the future is, for many of us, a big question mark? I have no neat and pat answers, but the purpose of this study is to be able to share our very different experiences and maybe come to some conclusions on these and related issues.

There are vast areas of religious life we could explore, but I would like to identify just two aspects which in my experience have enormous significance for communities, their self-understanding and their future existence. One issue is more general and theoretical: the relationship, and frequently the tension, between the needs of the individual and those of the community. The other looks at particular and practical instances of this: the sometimes unreal expectations of newcomers to the community regarding what Sandra Schneiders, in an excellent paper (it is now nearly thirty years since her classic *New Wineskins: Re-Imagining Religious Life Today* first appeared, but it is still a valuable voice for religious of all varieties), refers to as 'being parented' and 'parenting' and also unreal expectations regarding intimacy in a religious community.[11] These are only some of the issues which surface regularly as problem areas in community life, but I think they are key ones.

Perfectae Caritatis rightly insists that 'the up-to-date renewal of institutes depends very much on the training of the members'.[12] Obviously appropriate renewal depends largely on new members coming to join us, bringing with them their own fresh insights but also being willing to accept the charism of the order or congregation and to be guided by the spirit which animated the founders and which, hopefully, they still find alive and dynamic among us today. However, the expectations of newcomers regarding community are frequently unrealistic and it is part of

---

[11] Ibid.
[12] *Perfectae Caritatis*, 18.

the discernment process of formation to help newcomers identify these unreal expectations and ground them in real life.

So here I offer what could be a few pointers, using the perspectives identified some twenty-five years ago by the American sociologists Charles Gerkin and Robert Bellah and colleagues that explore the issues of individualism versus society.[13] These contemporary issues have been transposed into an ecclesial and even a liturgical context by the liturgist, J. Neil Alexander.[14] The work of all these American scholars regarding fragmentation, individualism and the community is related to the research of Paul McPartlan, which in turn explores and develops the thinking of Henri de Lubac found in his groundbreaking work *Catholicism*, which McPartlan describes as 'a sustained attack upon individualism in Christianity'.[15]

Neil Alexander, quoting Bellah, makes a very telling distinction between 'communities' and 'lifestyle enclaves'. Bellah claims the following characteristics of a 'community' as being an inclusive whole, where public and private aspects of life are interdependent and are celebrated as such, and the different callings of all the members are recognised and acknowledged. On the other hand, in a 'lifestyle enclave' the individuals are fragmented (i.e. they only partially invest themselves in the group), the group has a clear but often narrow, understanding of itself and its *raison d'être* and thus its agenda is also fragmented. It is often oblivious, or at least negative and antagonistic, to those

---

[13] Charles Gerkin, *Widening the Horizons: Pastoral Responses to a Fragmented Society* (Westminster: John Knox Press, 1986); Robert Bellah et al., *Habits of the Heart: Individualism and Commitment in American Life* (Berkley: University of California Press, 1985).
[14] Neil Alexander, 'In Time and Community: Individualism and the Body of Christ', in J. Neil Alexander, ed., *Time and Community: In Honour of Thomas J. Talley* (Washington: The Pastoral Press, 1990), pp. 294–5.
[15] Henri de Lubac, *Catholicism: Christ and the Common Destiny of Man* (London: Burns & Oates, 1962), translation of *Catholicisme: Les Aspects Sociaux du Dogme* (Paris: Cerf, 1947); Paul McPartlan, *The Eucharist Makes the Church: Henri de Lubac and John Zizioulas in Dialogue* (Edinburgh: T & T Clark, 1993), p. 14.

outside its boundaries, while being segmented and narcissistic within itself. Alexander emphasises what is perhaps the most telling observation:

> In the enclave, the unity of purpose is the result of the collection of persons of the same position. In the community, certain values, viewpoints or positions belong first to the group and are then shared by those who are members of it.[16]

I think the significance of the work of these sociologists for religious communities is very obvious. While much emphasis is rightly placed today on individual responsibility, if individuals only 'partially invest themselves' in the group, the result will be that they feel themselves to be on the fringe of the life of the community and they will experience a sense of marginality and alienation, which is self-perpetuating because of their lack of genuine commitment and the community will be fragmented. Life becomes a vicious circle.

One cannot help but wonder if some of the more 'traditional' new religious communities and movements, who appear to be cultivating a return to a pre-Vatican II mentality in their adherents, fit Alexander's and Bellah's description of 'lifestyle enclaves'. They appear to have a 'clear but narrow under-standing' of their calling and their purpose and they can be 'negative and antagonistic' towards those outside their boundaries. Is their 'unity of purpose' the result of the coming together of people who already hold the same, possibly extreme, positions, whereas in a true community the uniting values and ideals belong first to the whole group which then shares its uniting factors with newcomers? How do we ensure that we offer true, authentic and genuine community and not merely a 'lifestyle enclave' to those interested in joining us? Can we identify some aspects of community life which can unite us in a healthy and positive way as an authentic community, rather than a 'lifestyle enclave'?

To try and make some concrete suggestions, the second area of community life to which I would like to direct attention,

---

[16] Alexander, 'In Time and Community', p. 295.

because of its significance for newcomers, is a practical development of the above: it is that of realistic expectations regarding the sharing of ideals and of experience at different levels of community life. Schneiders lists some of the values and needs which it is realistic and legitimate for members of a community to expect to share with each other: 'worship, prayer and faith sharing in the spiritual sphere, the supplying of mutual assistance, support, affirmation, the space to be oneself and to grow reasonable, caring confrontation when necessary, and a sense of belonging, interdependence, and friendship in the psychological sphere.'[17] She comments rightly, that communities will vary very much in their respective ability to supply these needs of their members, particularly, I would suggest, as communities grow older and smaller, but these are real, genuine and legitimate needs which any community can be expected to meet at least in some measure. A community can legitimately be evaluated in terms of its ability and willingness to function in this way and offer support and encouragement to its members.

However, there are other functions which a religious community should not be expected to exercise. If the members of that community are adult women, they should not expect to be 'parented'. Schneiders lists some of the ways in which it is possible to demand, either implicitly or explicitly, to be parented: 'hypochondria, cultivated ineptitude, the inability to be alone, the refusal to master the ordinary skills of adult living such as cooking, moodiness and emotional instability.' All these are manipulative demands for 'endless parenting', notice and attention, and are inappropriate in an adult community. The other side of the coin is that adult religious should not expect to fulfil the function of a 'parent'. By our commitment to a celibate way of life we have made the sacrifice of all forms of parenthood, not just the physical. So the 'need to run the lives of others, the conviction that we know what is good for them, the need to fuss over them, intrusion into the private affairs of others, the need to impose our own little rules of the house on others', all these

---

[17] Schneiders, 'The Changing Shape and Function of Community Life', p. 248.

betray the religious who has not come to terms with the sacrifice involved in celibacy. 'The only appropriate way to deal with fellow community members is as one autonomous adult with another.'

In addition, perhaps most tellingly of all, Schneiders identifies a third need which cannot legitimately be met in a religious community. Although religious life is sometimes compared to a 'family', this can produce unreal expectations in that no religious community can, or should try to replicate what Schneiders calls 'the intimacy and total mutuality characteristic of marriage partners'. She comments, 'The expectation that community life will be an experience of totally fulfilling intimacy' produces what for many can be 'one of the most frequent and bitter disappointments of some young religious today'.[18] Although religious life can reasonably be expected to provide 'mutuality, support, participation, belonging, personal affirmation and appreciation, opportunities for self-development, and gradually increasing responsibility for the shared enterprise', Schneiders points out that the satisfaction of the human need for intimacy, in spite of the legitimate expectation of mutuality and friendship, 'cannot be realistically demanded of one's immediate community' and 'one cannot realistically expect to experience all these values in an intense way at all times'.[19] The community does not exist solely to supply the psychological needs of the members. Deep friendships often grow up and flourish in religious communities, but this takes much time, and newcomers frequently do not appreciate this.

But in spite of all the problems and the difficulties which still remain (and, I suspect, will always remain, because they are inevitable whenever human beings live together at very close quarters), it is vital that we ourselves have a firm and strong belief in the sacramental value and significance of community life. We have the words of Christ himself to inspire and encourage us: 'Where two or three are gathered together in my name, there am

[18] Ibid., p. 249.
[19] Ibid., p. 256.

I in the midst of them' (Matthew 18:20). Our religious communities present to the world the Body of Christ in microcosm. We can become so used to the phrase 'Real Presence' as referring to that of Christ in the Eucharist that we can overlook the other forms of 'presence' which are equally real, and his presence among Christians gathered together in his name is nowhere more 'real' than in our religious communities, activated and actualised by our daily sharing in the Eucharist.

So I return to the passage from *Perfectae Caritatis* with which I began, to show the apostolic and eschatological value Vatican II gave to religious community life and which it is ours to actualise:

> A community gathered together as a true family in the Lord's name enjoys his presence (cf. Mt 18:20), through the love of God which is poured into their hearts by the Holy Spirit (cf. Rom. 5:5). For love sums up the law (cf. Rom. 13:10) and is the bond which makes us perfect (cf. Col. 3:14); by it we know we have crossed over from death to life (cf. 1 Jn 3:14). Indeed, the unity of the brethren is a symbol of the coming of Christ (cf. Jn 13:35; 17:21) and is a source of great apostolic power.

This sacramental value of our religious life lived in community is both our privilege and our glory, our gift to the church, and it can also be our daily examination of conscience. I hope you will forgive a Poor Clare if I quote the words of our foundress, Clare of Assisi, who wrote the following, 'I hold you to be a support for the frail and failing members of Christ's ineffable Body.' Though Clare wrote these words to an individual, Agnes of Prague, I think they can with equal truth be applied to our communities. In ways, both temporal and spiritual, both material and transcendent, by our prayer and our example, our practical help and our encouragement, our lives of prayer and of apostolic endeavour, we are called to support the frail and failing members of the Body of Christ by making that Body ever more visibly present in the world through the witness that our lives of love in community gives to the world.

Community is a basic human need. Our religious communities provide centres of hope, support, friendship, comfort, a sense of belonging and a spiritual home to countless people. For some years I was secretary to the Association of British Contemplatives and then on the Poor Clare Federation Council and both of these involved visiting and staying in other monasteries. Wherever I went I found little groups of people centred around each community for whom that community was their spiritual home. They found in their link with that community, an identity, a feeling of belonging, a focus for their prayer. We experienced this very vividly in my own house a few years ago, when we inaugurated associate members, lay people who wanted to have a spiritual bond with our community. They tell us that this link with us has totally transformed life for many of them. It has given them this spiritual home and sense of belonging.

Reflection Questions

1. Community is the area in religious life where there have been some of the biggest changes since Vatican II. How do we understand these changes?

2. Community is the area in religious life in which some of our biggest challenges lie today. How do we face those challenges?

3. Community is the area in religious life where some of our most effective witness for the future lies. How are we going to live this out?

6

Half Way Home:
A Reflection from a Mendicant on Religious as Dialogue in Honour of Fifty Years of Perfectae Caritatis

Brian Terry SA

An epic journey

Homer sang at the beginning of the Odyssey,

> Tell me, O Muse, of the man of many devices, who wandered full many ways after he had sacked the sacred citadel of Troy. Many were the men whose cities he saw and whose mind he learned, aye, and many the woes he suffered in his heart upon the sea, seeking to win his own life and the return of his comrades.[1]

Reflecting on fifty years of *Perfectae Caritatis*, I came to marvel at the journey itself and how it has seemed so 'epic'. I began to think of heroes and heroines and the trials and tribulations of communities seeking to renew and adapt so as 'to win their own life' and that of their members. In half a century so much has happened as a result of the call to renew and adapt religious life. We as religious have studied ourselves, written new constitutions, debated and prayed for our life together. To hear members of our communities remember the Second Vatican Council and tell the stories of these fifty years just seemed like an 'Odyssey'. And it seems as if our Odyssey is not over as so many seem to feel we are before another crisis of religious life. What follows will be a reflection on some of the issues we still face as we look at

---

[1] Homer, *The Odyssey*, trans., A. T. Murray, (London: William Heinemann, 1919), 1:1.

declining numbers and closings of ministries and ask where we are on this continuing epic journey.

An epic story is one which usually centres around one heart, one person's wondrous story. For most of us, our founder's is the story of the heart we know the best. In some moment of crisis, our founders were raised up by God to an epic journey in order to dialogue with the world 'God loved so much' and renew God's definition of dignity. For one who listens to the stories of Francis, this is certainly his literal quest. The people of God were suffering and the institutions of the *Civitas* and the church did not hear the voice of the poor. The walled medieval cities became the walled medieval mindset which closed out any challenge to the unjust systems which reduced people to a commodity. Francis asks all who walk with him, to 'go out'. The penitent must go out, of their place, of their comfort zone and, even in the world's eye, 'out of their mind', as 1 Corinthians 4:10 reminds us, as 'fools for Christ'. The journey is one of *meta-noia*, of going out of or beyond (*meta*) the mindset (*noia*) of a monologue of crisis to a dialogue with the other about God. Today, with so much discussion of crises of the economy, the church and religious life, is our epic journey to lead us to 'go out of our mind'?

An epic dialogue

A hallmark of the epic journey is usually a memorable dialogue. If we look again to Homer's Odyssey, one of the more famous moments of crisis is when the Cyclops had captured Ulysses. The introduction of a person in an epic was one of the most important moments. The Cyclops, who was about to dine on Ulysses and friends, was driven to ask, 'Who are you?' The crafty Ulysses, desperate to keep the pre-dinner conversation going as long as possible to ward off his imminent death answers, 'No-man is my name, No-man do they call me, my mother and my father, and all my comrades as well.' For Ulysses, the dialogue is his escape from a very real crisis. And Ulysses, the man of many devices, escapes his crisis through this powerful moment. First, ironically talking the Cyclops to sleep and then, eventually blinding the one-eyed Cyclops. To guarantee his escape, he had further crippled the Cyclops from even calling for help by giving to him an ambiguous name. When asked by his comrades who to apprehend, the wounded Cyclops cries out 'No-man has blinded me!' Those cyclops who could see were searching for 'No-man'.

In a metaphorical way the importance of good dialogue is brought to light. However, might this crisis from the epic have a few challenges to the present day state of religious men and women? Might the image of religious be captured by a 'one-eyed', singular, superficial perspective in our world, a world which chooses success over faithfulness? And what name have we given to ourselves in our world? Perhaps the name we call ourselves is so ambiguous it even fools ourselves and confuses the world? Might the world be calling for 'no-one', and there is 'no-one' to respond? Aren't we as religious men and women called to be a religious dialogue with the world about God?

Towards some-one religious
We have heard how St Thomas Aquinas cautions us, 'An error about the creature causes an even more mistaken theology, and distracts human minds from God in whom they ought to direct their faith.'[2] To dialogue about God with the world, we must first see and name ourselves. The Second Vatican Council called for vowed religious to name themselves in *Perfectae Caritatis*, while at the same time we heard a similar question from *Gaudium et Spes*.[3] Joseph Ratzinger reminded us that 'the whole Pastoral Constitution might therefore be described in this light as a discussion between Christian and unbeliever on the question who and what man really is', and for our part, who and what a vowed

---

[2] *ScG* II, 3, 1.
[3] To refer to a person in vows, for the sake of argument, I would prefer to use the name 'vowed' religious, because it aligns with an affirmation to be made below. A religious is one who chooses to 'vow'. They are not passively consecrated. In another place, I have treated the necessary element of consent for a person's identity and ability to enter into a sacrament.

religious is.[4] Yet, thirty years later in 1994, David Tracy told us, 'We live in an age which cannot name itself.'[5] 'Someone' needs an answer. And, coming to understand what 'true dialogue' is will help us explain who we are.

The challenge of the vowed religious, the heart of the church, the ambassador of reconciliation, is to encounter the other and be a dialogue with the people of God, to invite them to go out of their mind. To arrive at that destination, I invite you to 'go out' and walk with me through a few propositions. First, the operational definition of the human is significantly different from the times of the Council but ironically more in line with it. We need a clear definition of ourselves, the subject, because 'true dialogue' today has a way to be an ever-renewing of our self. Second, politics and debates confuse our understanding of the word 'dialogue'. We must even explore what 'true dialogue' means. It can serve as a vehicle to naming ourselves and our mission. Finally, Johannes B. Metz in his book *Followers of Christ: Perspectives on the Religious Life* states that a religious community will survive, *ars vivendi*, if it can transmit its foundation and charism to the first generation after the death of the founder.[6] If this is true, it is a rare moment in time where all religious life of the church which existed at the Council can be seen as just beginning this crucial phase, as we move past the first generation after the Council with renewed constitutions and identities. We all are struggling to say who we are to ourselves and to the next generation. If we live in a time in which we cannot name ourselves, name our communities, and all of us are collectively living in a 'new community', is there any wonder that we speak of a time of epic 'crisis'?

---

[4] Joseph Ratzinger, 'The Dignity of the Human Person', in Herbert Vorgrimler, ed., *Commentary on the Documents of Vatican II* (New York: Herder & Herder, 1969), vol. 5, p. 118.

[5] David Tracy, *On Naming the Present: God, Hermeneutics, and Church* (Maryknoll: Orbis, 1994), p. 3.

[6] Johannes B. Metz, *Followers of Christ: Perspectives on the Religious Life*, trans. Thomas Linton (London: Burns & Oates, 1978), 12 ff.

Incarnation: a snapshot of the times: In Medias Res
When *Perfectae Caritatis* was written, we were in the middle of a
lot of different things. A strong sign of the times was the refining
of the definition of the human. If the task of a religious is first to
name themselves, we were given a task to name ourselves in a
very fluid time which was changing our understanding of
ourselves. In order to build the proposal that 'religious be
dialogue', we need to look at a brief development of how the
human who seeks to communicate becomes a human of dialogue.

Who do you say the human is?
In 1959, Thomas J. Deegan and a few of his friends announced
the 1964 World's Fair in New York to celebrate the 300th
anniversary of the founding of New York with the theme 'Peace
Through Understanding: Man's Achievement on a Shrinking
Globe in an Expanding Universe'. The search for a *Weltanschauung*, a world view, was rampant.[7] The iconic symbol of the
World's Fair was to be the Unisphere, a globe with three rings on
it to represent trajectories of the first two men in space, Yuri
Gagarin and John Glenn, and the Telstar Satellite, the first
communications satellite. The world was marvelling at two men
who had been the furthest to 'go out' of most of people's world

---

[7] '"*Weltanschauung*" is, I am afraid, a specifically German notion, which
it would be difficult to translate into a foreign language. If I attempt to
give you a definition of the word, it can hardly fail to strike you as
inept. By *Weltanschauung*, then, I mean an intellectual construction
which gives a unified solution of all the problems of our existence in
virtue of a comprehensive hypothesis, a construction, therefore, in
which no question is left open and in which everything in which we
are interested finds a place. It is easy to see that the possession of such
a *Weltanschauung* is one of the ideal wishes of mankind. When one
believes in such a thing, one feels secure in life, one knows what one
ought to strive after, and how one ought to organize one's emotions
and interests to the best purpose.' Sigmund Freud, *New Introductory
Lectures on Psycho-Analysis* (1933), *Scribd.* [online resource], 10 May
2010, <http://www.scribd.com/doc/31127291/7/LECTURE-XXXV>

view along with a device which gives us the means to speak to one another anywhere on the world. Communication came to define the times and even the human. The human was being heralded for the achievements humanity had made. The human doing was replacing the centre of the human being.

At the same time, in January of 1959, Pope John XXIII announced his plans to call a worldwide ecumenical council. A few years later, on 31 October 1962, John XXIII pressed a button from the Vatican which started the pile drivers to begin construction on the Vatican Pavilion four thousand miles away in Flushing Meadows, NY just two weeks after opening the Second Vatican Council. *Ecclesia* and technology: we marvelled at the events which were taking place and saw ourselves from a new, broader perspective which brought a euphoric hope, a hope which stood in dark contrast to the generation before, where so many felt forgotten in a series of horrifying wars and direct or indirect attempts at the annihilation of peoples. Jewish people, Armenian people, Japanese people, Native American people, African people all had tried to call out from imprisonment in a brother or sister's voice. But few heard it.

In 1963 John XXIII seemed to speak of the crisis for the voiceless in *Pacem in Terris*, echoing the words of Pius XII's 1943 Christmas message,

> Any well-regulated and productive association of men in society demands the acceptance of one fundamental principle: that each individual man is truly a person. ... As such he has rights and duties, which together flow as a direct consequence from his nature. These rights and duties are universal and inviolable, and therefore altogether inalienable.[8]

We may find it hard to believe, we were about to put a person on the moon but there was no agreed definition in the world of every human as a person. We had suffered the theories of polygenesis and eugenics which gave us justifications for slavery and superior races and genocide. The Second Vatican Council, through *Gaudium et Spes*, would remind us of the 8th Psalm's

---

[8] John XXII, *Pacem in Terris*, 9.

question, 'Who is man you are mindful of him?' The authors were searching to describe the human person through the human's experience and a dialogue with the modern world. The definition of a human would be forever linked to dialogue. And as will be explored below, true dialogue means we are changed by the encounter. Who changes whom?

What does this have to do with the religious of today? The nature of religious life is much more about who we are than what we do, but we so quickly describe ourselves by how we work, pray, dress and live. A fun question to ask a room full of Christians is, 'If we are created in the image and likeness of God, who do we look like?' The almost uniform answer is Jesus Christ, when a fuller answer is the Trinity. Too often we keep our image of God as a person, and not the Trinity. And, as a default, we reduce our identity to be an individual of the Trinity and not the radical relationship of the Trinity as a whole, the radical relationship of dialogue which imprints us with a need to be in relationship, a radical relationship of faithfulness. The reduction of our image to an individual of the Trinity only promotes an individualism which fractures a community into a group who coexist in the same space to do our own thing. We must be a dialogue because it is who we are, persons in radical faithfulness to the Other and one another.

True dialogue with the other

> For the prime characteristic of Christian faith is that it is faith in God. Furthermore, that this God is someone who speaks, someone to whom man can speak. The Christian God is characterized by revelation, that is, in the words and deeds in which he addresses man. And the goal of revelation is man's response in word and deed which thus expands revelation into a dialogue.[9]

As the then Cardinal Ratzinger reminded us, the human could dialogue with God. Paul Ricoeur's linguistic work on the

---

[9] Joseph Cardinal Ratzinger, *Feast of Faith* (San Francisco: Ignatius, 1986), p. 16.

philosophy of dialogue will interestingly make this the most necessary part of identity. The recent linguistic turn in philosophy shows how true dialogue is what forms and informs the self. Through words, we would come to an understanding. Through understanding, we would come to meaning. Unfortunately, many times we are just trying to pay attention to one another or spend a lot of time just communicating information. For meaning to form and transform the self, we need true dialogue, a meeting of two subjects who each see the other as like oneself. This is dialogue.

Ricoeur would stand on the shoulders of great philosophers such as Martin Buber, Jürgen Habermas and Hans-Georg Gadamer and show how they came to understand the human as a sum of the horizons of all the people they had met; each of those also being a sum of horizons, a sum of great dialogues which formed the self.

> The horizon of the present is being continually formed, in that we have continually to test all our prejudices. An important part of that testing is the encounter with the past and the understanding of the tradition from which we come … In a tradition this process of fusion is continually going on, for the old and new continually grow together to make something of living value, without either being explicitly distinguished from the other.[10]

'True' dialogue would be seen as the interaction between two subjects who had integrated many previous dialogues, not one subject and the other object, who affect and change one another by the experience of this exchange. This would be called 'intersubjectivity'. This exchange would bring understanding which then gives life meaning. And if the one with whom a person is dialoguing is God, we fuse our horizons with God.

Ricoeur would push us further to understand how the human is a product of dialogue as an exchange, an exchange of gifts. Yet the exchange was not just a marketplace consumerism, not just 'gift/regift'. Ricoeur challenges us to see the central moment shift from the giving or the re-giving to the 'receiving in *agape*'. And,

---

[10] Hans-Georg Gadamer, *Truth and Method* (New York: Seabury, 1975), p. 273.

receiving is twofold. 'Receiving then becomes the pivotal category, in that the way in which the gift is accepted determines the way in which the person who receives the gift will feel obliged to give something in return.'[11] However, as in the gifts of God, there were times when things were given in *insouciance*, *agape*, with no expectation of return. At times the receiver cannot reciprocate. They are left with only one response. 'A word comes to mind that we mentioned earlier in passing: gratitude.'[12] Since *agape* does not care if there is a return, the gratitude of the receiver is where we discover the meaning of 'without price'. In the true dialogue, the true exchange, the human is constantly immersed in gratitude.

To sum up what may seem as two digressions, to speak of a vowed religious as dialogue intends a radical living of the Trinitarian image of the human who, because of a great gratitude, engages the church and world in a dialogue. The religious is engaging in a radical choice to see all as like themselves, of equal dignity. 'Someone' needs to be in dialogue with the world. The vowed religious is already a radical dialogue and therefore must be a dialogue with the world.

O happy crisis

As said above, the majority of founders of religious communities came into an understanding of the charism given to them by God in a time of crisis. Moreover, their own personal crises often honed the gift. If we see ourselves at a time of crisis, isn't this where we are supposed to be? Br Sean Sammon repeatedly emphasises in his workshops and books how we are called to be 'faithful not successful'. The contributions above challenge the vowed religious to rename their identity through a faithful dialogue. In what follows I would like to build on the dialogue of identity further with a few points for us to ponder, starting from the ground up.

---

[11] Paul Ricoeur, *The Course of Recognition*, trans. David Pellauer, Institute for Human Sciences Vienna Lecture Series, (Cambridge, MA: Harvard University Press, 2007), p. 243.
[12] Ibid.

Getting at the imaginary roots

To begin, we return to a version of our original question in order to escape from a one-eyed monster who seeks to eat us alive, 'Who do you say that you are?' Famous for his works on identity, Victor Turner asks us to look to the roots of how we 'imagine' ourselves.

> Root paradigms are certain consciously recognized (though not consciously grasped) cultural models in the heads of the main actors. ... These have reference not only to the current state of social relationships existing or developing between actors, but also to the cultural goals, means, ideas, outlook, currents of thought, patterns of belief, and so on, which enter into those relationships, interpret them, and incline them to alliance or divisiveness. ... Paradigms of this fundamental sort reach down to irreducible life stances of individuals, passing beneath conscious prehension to a fiduciary hold on what they sense to be axiomatic values, matters literally of life and death.[13]

To understand ourselves is to understand our root paradigms. It leads us to ask, what is the root paradigm of religious life? We all know how our founders were people who could make Christ present in our world and invite the people of God to transformation. In the case of Francis, he sought such unity with Christ, the miracle story tells of how the seraphim appeared before him and when the angel left, Francis had the signs of the crucifixion. In my interpretation of the story, Francis became so prayerful he became prayer and the dialogue became so intense, his whole body spoke of Christ. The seraphim did not come to harm Francis by wounding him, God is not violent. The seraphim came to do what Francis could not do alone, to remove the last veil of his separation from Christ and allow the Christ from within to 'be' always, so the world could see the Christ. Fr Paul Francis Wattson, the founder of my community, the Franciscan Friars of the Atonement, could no longer live the division of war in his world or the fracture of Christ's church. Fr Paul's life was given to the world so we could make room for unity.

---

[13] Victor Turner, *Dramas, Fields, and Metaphors: Symbolic Action in Human Society* (Ithaca: Cornell University Press, 1974), p. 64.

I would like to propose we not just 'do' dialogue, but realise how we become it. In the story of Creation, God separates the light from the darkness, the water from the land using the creative verb *bārā*. In the space created, the inbetween, God places the human. For the religious, the vows can be seen in these creative terms. We separate any tendency to see the other as object, as a choice for a 'radical intersubjectivity'. We ask to live in a radical state of forgiveness, a radical state of where God has made room and nothing separates us from God. We ask God to make room for a future away from our tendencies to exploit and abuse the other. The *bārā*, the separation, the 'inbetween', is religious life. It is the creative dialogue of God. It is not a separation from the world, but a separation from divisiveness in the world and the disobedience to God's will. It is a radical unity with God, extended to the other so the other always remains a subject. We need to explore an 'in-between' theology for vowed religious life.

Dialoguing with a future
In the book and play *The Search for Signs of Intelligent Life in the Universe* written by Jane Wagner and acted by the comedienne Lily Tomlin, one of the confused characters who is going through a midlife crisis says, 'When I was young, I always wanted to grow up be someone … but now I see I should have been a little more specific.' While we are necessarily open to the mystery of the Spirit working in our lives, we need to reflect on our image of ourselves to understand how we see ourselves in the image and likeness of the Trinitarian God, and be a little more specific. From this, we are gifted with a wondrous dialogue which becomes a celebratory liturgy of our life in the image and likeness of the Trinity. The divine dialogue with God, the dialogue with ourselves and the dialogue with the world is who we are. These are not 'things' we do. We need to radically 'be dialogue' in our context of today.

> For the vast majority of people in the Western world today, the presumed hermeneutic of these church and theological leaders … has no meaning whatsoever. In other words, the hermeneutic that these church people use as a tool for meaning has become,

for a large part of the third-millennium population of this world, meaningless.[14]

In the fifty years since the authors penned *Perfectae Caritatis*, we have come a long way. We need to live a radical subject–subject life. It stands in great contrast to today's superficial world hallmarked by a flutter of impersonal tweets and texts which bruises and cheapens the depth of our very selves and our relationships with one another. We need an ongoing renewal of our faithfulness to the evangelical counsels seen as an ongoing dialogue with our God, our religious communities and our world. The world needs to hear of the divine dialogue of forgiveness, where God extends the creative separation that resulted in creation to the separation of ourselves from the divisions we have made. We need to be separated from our divisions and the sometimes limiting and destructive pasts we have. We need the very creative separation for us to once again have a future, a wonder-filled future where we can dare to hope, where we can find our fullness in being a child of God, growing each day in image and likeness of our God. St Francis sent out his followers 'to preach the Word of God, and sometimes use words'. We can never justify why we keep a charism given to our founders separated unto ourselves. Do we religious not see and hear the crisis? Who will speak of the love and reconciliation of God? Let's talk.

Reflection Questions

1. 'The divine dialogue with God, the dialogue with ourselves and the dialogue with the world is who we are.' What do you understand this to mean in the context of religious life?

2. What do you understand by 'the root paradigm of religious life'? Is there a particular 'root paradigm' connected with the founder or charism of your congregation? How is it lived in the present day?

---

[14] Kenan B. Osborne, *Christian Sacraments in a Postmodern World: A Theology for the Third Millennium* (New York: Paulist Press, 1999), p. 56.

7

Religious 'Praying Daily' as Church

Thomas R. Whelan CSSp

The liturgy of the church belongs to the entire church, of which religious form part.[1] The liturgical life of the church is integral to the 'mission of God' in which the church (including professed religious) is obliged to participate by virtue of baptism. These two statements are inseparable and create the context in which we must discuss the Liturgy of the Hours and religious life.

WHAT IS THE PRESENTING PROBLEM?

We love the idea of the Liturgy of the Hours, of 'praying the psalms', of gathering together to offer praise and glory to God and to intercede, but in practice have never made much of a fist of it. In an early writing of his, the late Monsignor J.D. Crichton said that the 'Church holds a high doctrine of the divine office, yet its practice must be said to be low'.[2] This statement expresses the kernel of the problem. Crichton's comment might go some way towards explaining why, anecdotally at least, it would seem

---

[1] The term 'religious' will be employed in a broad sense to refer to consecrated religious as well as to members of societies and associations of Apostolic Life. Monastic and contemplative communities normally follow a different tradition of praying the Hours, and their specific situations will not be considered in this reflection except in a general way. However, as the underlying theological principles apply to all, it is hoped that they too might find something here of interest to them.

[2] J.D. Crichton, *The Church's Worship: Considerations on the Liturgical Constitution of the Second Vatican Council* (London: Geoffrey Chapman, 1966), p. 187.

a significant number of priests and religious do not feel that the Liturgy of the Hours is as inviting a prayer form as they would like it to be. Busy ministries and pastoral engagements often become reasons for its less-than-regular use, and it can be seen by those who are canonically bound to this form of prayer as a burden and an obligation that must, at best, be fulfilled, even if minimally. Unfortunately a small number of clergy and religious have all but abandoned a regular use of Daily Prayer. Some larger religious communities frequently maintain a daily assembly at morning and evening for prayer, and most use the current Roman Office or a variation of it. A few communities, not finding in the Hours a way of praying that satisfies their deeper spiritual needs or the nourishment required for their apostolic ministry, create forms of prayer based loosely on the Roman structure. Other religious substitute Daily Prayer with creative forms which owe little to the received liturgical form.

In contrast to this, there are individual priests and religious communities, frequently parish based, who desire to make of the Hours a common prayer with and in the local church. Their aspiration is that Daily Prayer with the local assembly (often associated with morning Eucharist) becomes a joyous 'duty of faith', to pray without ceasing as behoves all the baptised, and a time when the concerns of the day and of the world can be placed before God as part of their song of praise.

It needs to be remembered that a small number of lay people pray parts of the daily Hours, especially Morning and Evening Prayer, on their own. Some parishes throughout the world celebrate Morning Praises, with or without the presence of their ordained pastor, before weekday morning Mass. In fact, the (Roman) *Directory for Sunday Celebrations in the Absence of a Presbyter* (1988) indicates a preference for the celebration of a form of Morning (or Evening) Prayer (which might include the Sunday readings assigned in the lectionary for Mass), when the community cannot celebrate the Eucharist.[3] All of this indicates

---

[3] On this see Thomas R. Whelan, 'Sunday Liturgies in the Absence of Eucharist', in Eugene Duffy, ed., *Parishes in Transition* (Dublin: Columba, 2010), pp. 179–207.

that there is an urgent pastoral need to find a way of returning the Hours to its daily and popular roots. The attractiveness of the simple but traditional forms of the Hours celebrated in Taizé also testifies to a desire and need for a form of regular, if not daily, common prayer.[4] The importance of both Morning Prayer and Evensong in the liturgical life of the Anglican Communion, as well as in other post-Reformation churches, attests to this.[5]

This chapter will focus on some of the deeper issues relating to an understanding of the Prayer of the Church. This will be done in the context of a post-conciliar vision of liturgy that needs to inform our communal and personal worship. Religious and institutes of apostolic life have done much over the past fifty years to renew their lifestyles and reform how they serve mission in the light of their charisms. All have been enthusiastic in the way they engaged with the theological reflections that emerged from the Council. Unfortunately, many have never fully embraced a post-conciliar liturgical theology that attempts to deepen a sense of liturgy that guided the reforms. In this regard, religious are no different from the wider church which has rarely moved beyond a surface-level implementation of liturgy reform. The work of deepening a sense of liturgy must continue.

In approaching the question we will take as a starting point the fact that the church has, since its earliest times, gathered each day to proclaim the marvels of God by using psalms, hymns and intercession. This ancient and living practice can, in a renewed

---

[4] See, for example, *Praise God: Common Prayer at Taizé*, Emily Chisholm, trans. (New York: Oxford University Press, 1977).

[5] These are to be found in *Common Worship: Services and Prayers for the Church of England* (London: Church House Publishing, 2000); and *The Book of Common Prayer ... According to the Use of the Church of Ireland* (Dublin: Columba Press / General Synod of the Church of Ireland, 2004). For a good introduction to the Anglican tradition of Daily Prayer, see John Gibaut, 'The Daily Office', in Charles Hefling and Cynthia Shattuck, eds., *The Oxford Guide to The Book of Common Prayer: A Worldwide Survey* (Oxford: OUP, 2006), pp. 451–9; and Paul Bradshaw and Simon Jones, 'Daily Prayer', in Paul Bradshaw, ed., *A Companion to Common Worship*, vol. 2 (London: SPCK, 2006), pp. 1–32.

form, help us deepen our sense of why we should pray daily, how this might be conceived ritually, and how it relates to the mission of God that we wish to serve in religious life. I end by proposing 'attitudes' to the Hours that may assist reflection on how religious could assess their 'praying daily' as church, so that their collective and individual lives and ministry are enhanced.

A LEGACY OF THE REFORM OF THE 'BREVIARY' AFTER VATICAN II
While a large number of people were involved in the discussions and study that shaped the reform of the Prayer of the Church after Vatican II, compromises were made that didn't allow some of the more important issues to be addressed. It was probably the least successful of all of the elements of the liturgical reform of the past fifty years. A wonderful *General Instruction on the Liturgy of the Hours* (*GILH*; found at the beginning of books of the Hours) presents a magnificent theology and spirituality of prayer.[6] Unfortunately the actual rite of the Hours does not seem to facilitate the 'joy' that is supposed to frame this liturgy.

Having said that, the reformed Liturgy of the Hours greatly improves on what went before. The older Office was simplified so as to address concerns brought to the Council floor about creating a form of prayer that would respond to the needs of clergy who are heavily engaged with busy pastoral schedules. The entire psalter, once prayed in a single week, is now prayed over a four-week cycle. A uniform structure was created for both Morning and Evening Prayer; a variety of hymns was provided; the invocations and intercessions composed are contemporary in tone and give expression to a social consciousness; there is an

[6] The following abbreviations will be used for frequently cited documents: *AG*: *Ad Gentes*: Decree on the Missionary Activity of the Church (1965); *GILH*: *General Instruction on the Liturgy of the Hours* (1971); *LG*: *Lumen Gentium*: Dogmatic Constitution on the Church (1964); *SC*: *Sacrosanctum Concilium*: Constitution on the Liturgy (1963). English translation taken from Austin Flannery, *Vatican Council II: Conciliar and Postconciliar Documents* (Dublin: Dominican Publications, 1998).

RELIGIOUS 'PRAYING DAILY' AS CHURCH

assortment of types of psalmody; a degree of flexibility is offered for adaptation to various circumstances; and a consciousness of the *veritas horarum* (the truth of the Hours) whereby prayer offered would respect the time of the day at which it is intended to be prayed. All of these modifications created clear lines and are to be commended.

So much for the structures. But what of the underlying issues? In his important work on the topic, Robert Taft states that the real concerns that the reform of the Office brings up are less to do with structural and ritual matters but rather with the deep-seated mentality that refused to make a clean break with the past. He presented his principal observations under three headings which can be summarised as follows.[7]

Despite the existence of research relating to the earlier forms of Daily Prayer in the church as well as the diverse traditions in the Eastern churches, the reform of the Hours after the Council seemed not to be aware of the earlier tradition, and concentrated instead on its own Roman tradition in its medieval form. This version of the Roman Office was already a hybrid form, mixing together elements of two earlier forms of Daily Prayer. These forms were developed around the parish or popular way of Daily Prayer, and around a longer and more meditative monastic form. The former (also known as the 'cathedral form') was simple in structure and was well suited to daily use in the local churches. Encapsulating a slightly different theology of Daily Prayer, the monastic form was longer, less accessible than the cathedral form, and was given to a more reflective approach to the psalms. The later Roman version of the Hours was a fusion of these with the monastic dominating. Its structures became more complex as time went on and this necessitated a number of reforms of the breviary over the centuries, mostly without any degree of success.

A close reading of the work of the groups involved with the post-conciliar reform led Taft to conclude that an 'overriding concern [was] to produce a book' for clergy and religious. This

---

[7] These are found in Robert Taft, *The Liturgy of the Hours in East and West: The Origins of the Divine Office and its Meaning for Today* (Collegeville: Liturgical Press, 1986), pp. 314–16.

clericalist vision of the Hours was informed by an ignorance of history, and a narrow post-medieval, Latin-church understanding of what the Hours were meant to be, not just historically, but also theologically. As a result of this, Taft notes, the reformed Hours 'bears a strong monastic stamp'. The contemplative dimension that it supplies will be of great benefit to clergy and religious, but it certainly was not designed to become a popular devotional liturgy which would appeal to a wider grouping of believers. 'But this skirts the real issue, which is whether the Liturgy of the Hours should be a prayer book for the clergy, or something more.'[8]

Taft concludes that, as a result of its continued clericalisation in the post-conciliar reform, the Hours ended up being retained as 'privatised' prayer. Celebrating the Hours with members of the local church was not the starting point for discussion but was, in fact, deemed to be the exception, even if 'desirable' (see *GILH* 27). The presumption was that most clerics and religious would continue to celebrate the Hours alone. A second issue that militated against any radical type of reform was that the recitation, particularly of the two principal Hours, continued to remain compulsory for clergy (see *GILH* 28, 29), and if necessary in private. This, in the opinion of one writer, 'has done more to undermine the whole pastoral thrust of the [*General Instruction*] that anything I know'.[9] The point here, of course, is that by making it compulsory for clergy, the writers of this document seemed to have forgotten that it is incumbent on all of the baptised to pray daily, without ceasing (1 Thessalonians 5:17).[10]

The privatisation of the Hours, not new in that it just perpetuated what had for centuries been the practice, cut into the heart of what was initially an ecclesial activity. There was no sustained sense in the membership of the reform working group

---

[8] Taft, *The Liturgy of the Hours*, p. 316.

[9] William G. Storey, 'The Liturgy of the Hours: Cathedral versus Monastery', *Worship* 50 (1976), pp. 50–71, p. 71. It was the sixteenth-century reforms of the Divine Office that first introduced this obligation on clergy.

[10] See also Luke 18:1; 21:36; Acts 6:4; Eph 6:18–20; Col 4:2.

that the Liturgy of the Hours was for the entire church. This refusal to make the more 'radical break', to which Taft refers, with what was the prevailing mentality regarding the clerical nature and preserve of the Office, also created unneeded and unhelpful challenges in returning to the Hours its communal and popular form. 'Behind this, of course, lies the more fundamental issue of Western liturgical privatisation and Eucharistic excess.'[11]

Many of the difficulties relating to the painfully slow acquisition of forms of Daily Prayer in the life of the church, are rooted in the reluctance of the working group to take as its starting point a sound appreciation of the early history of the Liturgy of the Hours, as well as to deal with the inherited privatisation of the Hours and its further clericalisation.

THEOLOGICAL AFFIRMATIONS RELATING TO THE PRAYER OF THE CHURCH

If we reflect on the long practice of the church at its Daily Prayer, we discover a number of affirmations that can be made in its regard. A brief consideration of these will help us to get an angle on how best we might approach praying the Prayer of the Church today.

Liturgy of the Hours flows from mission

Because it is liturgy, the Liturgy of the Hours is 'apostolic' to its core. Its claim to be 'apostolic' is not based on an historical assertion, but rather a theological one. Church happens because of the proclamation of the Reign of God which was summed up in the life and ministry of Jesus of Nazareth. From apostolic times, the prayer and assembly of Christians served to recall the memory of Jesus, and in these gatherings he became 'known to them in the breaking of the bread' (Luke 24:35). The church was born from the desire to participate in the life, death and resurrection of Christ, and from the desire of those baptised to

---

[11] Taft, *The Liturgy of the Hours in East and West*, p. 316. Taft is referring to the fact that until Eucharist came to be celebrated daily the Liturgy of the Hours was considered to be *the* Daily Prayer of the church.

proclaim this liberating life of God's reign to others. The church does not exist for itself, but 'for the life of the world' (John 6:51). The ultimate purpose of the Liturgy of the Hours cannot be understood apart from this.

To pray the Liturgy of the Hours outside of the context of the mission of God is to relegate it to the realm of private piety and devotion. It may serve us well in our private prayer and become a source of piety and nourishment (as recommended by *SC* 90 and *GILH* 28), but as the Prayer of the Church, it relates, of necessity, to the mission of God.[12]

Liturgy of the Hours is a participation in the paschal mystery
Probably the most important insight found in the Liturgy Constitution is that liturgy is a participation in and an exercise of the paschal mystery of Christ (see especially *SC* 5–6) and the Prayer of the Church is no exception. This means that, in our praying the Hours, we are engaging with salvific reality in the death and resurrection of Christ. This implies incarnation, the enfleshment of God in our midst, the Resurrection, Ascension and Pentecost, that part of the Resurrection narrative that makes explicit for us the Trinitarian involvement in our salvation. It also speaks of the 'now-ness', the actuality of God's continuing salvific and active presence in the life of the world through the Spirit, and that we are now living in the 'last times', the *eschaton*. Christ can be identified with the reign which he preached. This same reign of God is only being acquired by us, painfully and slowly, as we, in our sinful stubbornness, grasp at it and simultaneously resist it. But come to fulfilment it must. The Kingdom is on a roll and can't be stopped by us, since we are aligned to it by virtue of our baptism. The paschal mystery is not a pious notion but an all-encompassing reality that pitches us into the very centre of a salvific dynamic that is nothing other than the heart of the Trinity.

---

[12] For a discussion of this see, Thomas R. Whelan, '"The Liturgy is Missionary:" Elements of a Fundamental Liturgical Theology of Mission', in Joe Egan and Brendan McConvery, eds., *Faithful Witness: Glimpses of the Kingdom: Essays in Honour of M. Anthony Geoghegan and Vincent MacNamara* (Dublin: Milltown Institute, 2005), pp. 357–75.

The Liturgy of the Hours thus reveals itself to be one of the ways in which we become part of the axis along which these 'eschatological times' moves on the journey towards its fullness in Christ (see 1 Corinthians 15).

Liturgy of the Hours is an ecclesial action

St Paul was the first to speak explicitly of the participation in the mystery of Christ's death and resurrection through baptism (see Romans 6:3–5), and this requires that the new life of baptism becomes the basis of the witness that we give. Because we are, together, one in and with Christ, we therefore are church. According to SC 6, the 'sublime sacrament of the whole church' is born from the saving death of Christ. Church, as it lives its baptismal vocation, becomes, in turn, a sacrament of Christ (see SC 5; LG 1, 48; AG 1), revealing Christ risen from the dead. In a real sense the church is a corporate extension in time, an embodiment of the paschal mystery which, in the symbolism of the Fourth Gospel, is born from the side of Christ on the cross.

That means that liturgy is not a private affair. It is ecclesial, a making present of the mystery of Christ (see SC 5–6). More importantly – and something that we Catholics are still struggling to learn – if liturgy is ecclesial it means that it is communal: i.e. it needs people. It makes no sense to do liturgy on our own. The normative mode of praying the Liturgy of the Hours is in church and with people (see SC 26–7).

Liturgy of the Hours is 'Prayer of the Church'

The pastoral practice of liturgy today lacks a firm sense of ecclesiology. We still tend to think of liturgical assembly quantitatively, as a collection of individuals, rather than communal project of salvation, a 'communion (koinonia) of life' in which we are saved not as 'individuals without any bond or link', but 'as a people' (LG 9).

The origins of what we today call, more formally, the Divine Office, are to be found in the daily assembly of baptised Christians who gathered at morning and evening to sing the praises of God and to intercede for the needs of the world. They constituted the local assembly gathered together at prayer, even if all of their members were unable to be present, obeying the evangelical mandate to 'pray without ceasing' (1 Thessalonians 5:17). This was the daily form of prayer, long before the medieval development that saw weekday Eucharist begin to take over and become the de facto form of daily worship. It was not the preserve of clergy, and the monastic tradition responded to the same desire to pray continuously in a slightly different way. What developed later in the West was a stylised and more complex form of the Hours that eventually became privatised and clericalised. There is a deep need today to reclaim this liturgical form and return it to the wider church, where it belongs.[13]

By outlining briefly the origins of the popular form of the Prayer of the Church, religious will learn that they do not pray the Hours *on behalf of* others in the sense that they do not *substitute* for the rest of the church, since they cannot relieve others of the biblical mandate to pray always. When Christians gather to pray the Hours, they *are* church assembled in prayer and they pray *with* the church. What religious do is fully ecclesial: they act as Body of Christ, a local manifestation of the church, in a particular form, and it is done *with* the church and *as church* rather than in its stead.

Liturgy of the Hours is an exercise of the priesthood of Christ
Whereas the monastic tradition seems to have considered the praying of the psalms in the Hours as a form of meditation on the Word, the more popular 'cathedral form' developed a sense that the Liturgy of the Hours were prayed with and as the voice of Christ, exercising his priesthood and (in and through the church's local assemblies) joining with him in offering praise to God and interceding for people (see SC 7, 83). The prayer of the assembly is thus not simply its own personal or communal prayer but the prayer of Christ, and therefore a participation in his eternal relationship with *Abba*.

---

[13] A very fine study of this is to be found in Arnaud Join-Lambert, *La liturgie des Heures par tous les baptisés. L'expérience quotidienne du mystère pascal*, Liturgia condenda 23 (Leuven: Peeters, 2009). This was reviewed by Patricia Rumsey in *Journal of Ecclesiastical History* 62 (2011), pp. 572–3.

Liturgy of the Hours involves intercession
Praying the Hours with Christ the eternal high Priest carries with it the obligation to offer prayer and intercession for the world. Embodying, however imperfectly, Christ's paschal mystery, we take on the cares of the world: from Syria to the melting ice cap; from refugee camps in various parts of Africa, Lebanon, and Asia, to soup kitchens in Dublin; from the seeking of resolutions to the current world financial crises to the care of disadvantaged and vulnerable people; from a concern for peoples of other faith traditions, to those who are victims of various forms of abuse in church quarters, not least victims of church's prevarication in their regard. All of this, in Christ, is the subject of our prayer as we offer praise and glorification to God and intercede 'for the life of the world' (John 6:51). Liturgy of the Hours never provides an escape from the world of which we are part, and monastic and enclosed communities take very seriously their obligation to bring before God, in the name of Christ, the concerns of the weakest, the abandoned, and the marginalised.

Liturgy of the Hours uses psalms
Liturgy has always employed the Hebrew psalter in various ways. In the more popular ancient form of the Hours, the psalms are read Christologically.[14] They are seen to be, if not the voice of Christ to the Father, then referring to Christ in his incarnational and salvific reality. In a very real sense the psalms reflect the most human sentiments in ways not true of any other form of prayer. Every emotion, from joy and delight to despair and anger, finds expression here.[15]

---

[14] On this, see Margaret Daly-Denton, 'Psalmody as "Word of Christ",' in Kathleen Hughes, ed., *Finding Voice to Give God Praise: Essays in the Many Languages of the Liturgy* (Collegeville: Liturgical Press, 1998), pp. 73–86; and her more recent, *Psalm-Shaped Prayerfulness: A Guide to the Christian Reception of the Psalms* (Dublin: Columba, 2010).
[15] A helpful piece here is that of Roland E. Murphy, 'Reading/Reciting the Psalms: Some Reflections', *Review for Religious*, 61 (2002), pp. 631–9.

The offering of praise to God is self-implicating. An authentic offering of praise and glorification to God requires that we see an echo of the psalms in the world around us, that by identifying with the *anawim*, God's poor, we equally identify with them in the streets outside of the chapel in which we pray.[16] Participation in the high priesthood of Christ is demanding.

Mission flows from Liturgy of the Hours

If we were able to begin with the assertion that 'Liturgy of the Hours flows from Mission', then the reverse is equally true. It is our service of the 'mission of God' that offers the *raison d'être* for our continued liturgical activity in the church community, and we must close that loop. The work of liturgy involves making us real participants in the mission task of God in Christ. The ultimate goal of all liturgy and mission is the worship of God at end-time when God will be all in all, and when we all, people from every tribe and tongue and nation, will feast with the lamb at the banquet, giving honour, glory and thanksgiving to God.

This is the context, focus and salvific sweep in which the Liturgy of the Hours is located and which it celebrates and makes actual. Liturgy makes present the salvific reality of the mystery of Christ, not merely as something from the past 'to be recalled' but as the continuing engagement that makes salvation real in the now (*hodie*). This actuality of the liturgical celebration makes of the liturgical assembly a place in which salvation is played out, negotiating with the reality in which this assembly lives and finds itself. Liturgy is never an escape from reality. If it becomes this, then it is not celebrated authentically. The assembly is not separated from world, as if world was the locus of evil or a place where God is absent. Assembly, if it is true to its Christian vocation, lives in 'world', and in fact, whether it likes it or not, helps to constitute the (local) world of which it is part. Its task, as leaven in society, is to transact with its environment so as to act as an instrument of transformation/evangelisation and to enable

---

[16] On the ethical aspect to liturgical celebration, see Thomas R. Whelan, 'Liturgical Formation: To What End?' *Anaphora* 2 (2008), pp. 1–20.

those assembled to become clearer as to what their collective life in Christ requires of them in their concrete situation.

SOME QUESTIONS TO BE CONSIDERED

Daily Prayer cannot be easily dismissed as simply being one form among others, to be chosen as one option among others. If it remains in the churches today, it is because it is seen to be of importance for the very sustenance of the life of the various communities and assemblies which create 'church' when they gather to pray.

Variety of charisms – one form of Daily Prayer?

The church today can boast of a great variety of religious institutes and associations of apostolic life. The early monastic, the medieval mendicant, the active apostolic religious of the counter-reformation church, as well as the more recent groupings of apostolic institutes, all represent different traditions, exhibit a variety of charisms, and serve the one mission of God in a diversity of ways. Not all are called to an extended Divine Office that is characteristic of contemplative communities. Some groups are caught up with active ministry, the upshot of which is that they are away from community chapel for much of the day, or they are called to a ministry in parish or other context that would permit a form of Daily Prayer involving members of the wider Christian community among whom they serve.

This begs the question as to whether we should expect the same liturgical structure of the Hours to be imposed equally on all. If it is true that, as anecdotal evidence suggests, there is and has been for some time, the makings of a crisis in how or whether religious pray the Prayer of the Church, then we need to be sufficiently courageous to deal with the issues involved, perhaps allowing the Liturgy of the Hours to become a repertoire for supplying us with models of Daily Prayer which will always reflect the best of tradition, but adapted to the charism and ministry of individual religious institutes today. It is interesting to note that the post-conciliar working groups dealing with the reform of the Liturgy of the Hours considered the introduction of a 'pastoral breviary' for use by those who had busy pastoral commitments. Monastic communities would use a different form of the Hours. There was also a call for a 'normative breviary' but with no agreement as to what this would look like.[17]

The tradition of the Hours in the church shows that there was a variety of forms and shapes that were modified and sculpted as thought appropriate, often by adding to existing structures, and thus requiring periodic reform. There may be a need today for active religious communities to assess the appropriateness of the current Roman form of the Divine Office.

Victims of history

Even fifty years after Vatican II and despite deep reflection on their traditions and charisms in the light of this Council, many religious still need to reflect on how a renewed understanding of liturgy might be embodied in their community and individual lifestyles. In the search for a renewed and contemporary expression of the founding charism, many groups have had difficulty in dealing with liturgical practices which reflected the times and pieties of an era in which they were founded, but which do not sit easily with a conciliar theology and practice of worship. Few groups succeeded in sifting the central intentions of a founder from their historical trappings and rereading these in the context of the Liturgy Constitution.

A renewed and renewing church must be faithful to the sense of liturgy which is found in the pages of the documents of Vatican II. Not that these have solved all of our liturgical and ecclesial problems! What they have done is offer to us, as a guide proposed by the church as it gathered in Council (and therefore not the arbitrary thoughts of a few wandering freaks enthused by liturgy), a sense of what worship might look like today. The importance of what the Council gave us is not simply the reformed rites but the deeper sense of what we are and who we

---

[17] See Stanislaus Campbell, *From Breviary to Liturgy of the Hours: The Structural Reform of the Roman Office, 1964–1971* (Collegeville: Liturgical Press, 1995), pp. 254–6. This book offers the best account written to date of the post-conciliar reform of the Liturgy of the Hours.

are as church when gathered in prayer. These principles did not emerge by capricious selection but from the study, reflection and prayerful consideration of history and an attempt at proposing a pastoral guide appropriate to contemporary needs. The Liturgy Constitution of Vatican II preferred to go with a biblical and theological understanding of the foundation of the church over an institutional founding that might place structure before mystery. In such an understanding the Holy Spirit has a chance to breathe.

All religious institutes are to some extent victims of ecclesial and liturgical history, especially those founded in medieval times onwards. Through their particular charism and ministry they continue to serve the one mission of God but the wrappings of this are often such that the rewritten constitutions guiding apostolic ministry in the early twenty-first century may need to be reshaped so as to be faithful to the deeper intentions that underpin the liturgical reform of the Council. For many groups this means that the role and place of the Liturgy of the Hours in their apostolic life needs to be re-evaluated in a way that both reflects the best of a conciliar understanding of liturgy and is faithful to the core of the charism that informs their lifestyle, and serves their ministry to the mission of God.[18]

RELIGIOUS AND THE LITURGY OF THE HOURS

This contribution began with a brief consideration of some 'presenting issues' among religious, a number of whom do not find the reformed Liturgy of the Hours to respond to their personal and apostolic needs. These 'presenting issues' were based on anecdote rather than scientific survey. However, if we

---

[18] By far the best writing relating to this question is that of Robert F. Taft, 'Liturgy in the Life and Mission of the Society of Jesus', in Keith Pecklers, ed., *Liturgy in a Postmodern World*, (London: Continuum, 2003), pp. 36–54. This might be more easily accessible to some readers in its slightly modified version in his, 'Jesuit Liturgy – An Oxymoron', *Worship* 84 (2010), pp. 38–70. While Taft's reflection relates to Jesuits, the underlying observations are valid for all religious institutes.

can accept their veracity, at least in broad terms, then it is clear
that not all is well with the way religious pray daily. For many,
the Liturgy of the Hours is not seen to be an inviting form of
prayer. It can be a burden unrelated to busy pastoral ministry, an
irrelevancy for which one finds it difficult to create time, a task
that needs to be finished each day, ideally in private. At best, for
some, its private recitation supplies a source for their own
spiritual nourishment, meditation and private prayer.

An honest appraisal of what expectations we have and what
'attitudes' inform our approach to the Office needs to be
contextualised by apostolic ministry, charism, the very best of the
traditions relating to the Liturgy of the Hours, contemporary
needs, and a profoundly ecclesial sense of liturgy.

Outline of a framework for understanding
All liturgy relates to the mission of God (*missio Dei*) and finds its
finality in leading the assembly to a deeper engagement with this
mission, whose ultimate destiny and purpose of the *missio Dei*
which we all serve is, according to St Augustine, to be found in
God alone.[19] The Book of Revelation describes this as an eternal
multicultural liturgy wherein an offering of praise, thanksgiving
and blessing is made to God in Christ. The liturgy we celebrate
now is at best a dim but nonetheless real foreshadowing of the
heavenly liturgy (see *SC* 8).

With this important orientation, we then need to affirm the
evangelical obligation, incumbent on all, to 'pray without
ceasing'. At the heart of being religious is the way it continues
this gospel mandate of unceasing prayer, which it does in its own
name as church and not as a substitute for the prayer of other
baptised persons. The Liturgy of the Hours is an exercise of the
priesthood of Christ in which we all have a share through
baptism. In and with Christ we carry the concerns of the world,
specifically those which relate to our daily ministry, and make
these part of the Christ's self-offering to the Father. Liturgy of the
Hours is an actualisation of Christ's paschal mystery, a
participation in his salvific work continuing on in the world in

---

[19] St Augustine, *Confessions*, Book I, 1:1.

our time. St Paul tells us that we must make of our bodies a living sacrifice, acceptable and pleasing to God (Romans 12:1). When Paul uses the language of cult and sacrifice, it is in reference to his own ministry and mission and never to liturgical ritual.[20] This ministry, for Paul, includes (liturgical) assembly, but is not constituted by it. To the extent that the Liturgy of the Hours relates to our ministry as religious, nourishing it and reflecting it, it is a priestly activity united with Christ's sacrificial self-offering. In this sense Daily Prayer pertains to the sacramental life of the church and can only be understood alongside other forms of liturgical prayer.

As liturgy, the Prayer of the Church is deeply ecclesial and is a public and not private form of prayer, a participation in the paschal mystery, which is also the source and origin of the church. The normal context of the Hours cannot be private recitation. There is a need to develop a spirituality that does not compart-mentalise liturgy, but that sees our assembling as constituting an essential but different form of service of God's reign alongside our active ministry, sleeping and eating. With these fundamental 'attitudes' in place, we can now consider briefly a few aspects of Daily Prayer in a way that will, hopefully, address concerns that some religious seem to have.

Simpler form of prayer
The reformed structure of the post-conciliar Hours is a huge improvement on what had gone before, and has much to recommend. However, it is still very monastic: it employs the full *cursus* of psalms and is more suited to groups who are able to meet regularly with a form of prayer that is rather complex.

A realisation that there are variations offered by the text and different ways of praying the psalms can be helpful, from the cathedral sense of chanting praise, in the name of Christ and in the name of the church, to the more monastic emphasis on the psalms as biblical text to be meditated on before turning to God in prayerful response (from which developed the Psalm Collects) and as part of the flow of a full day which aspires to be 'a

---

[20] See Whelan, 'The Liturgy is Missionary', pp. 367–9.

prayerful, continuous communion with the living God and with one another in him'.[21] On the other hand, active religious with a busy pastoral schedule are probably better served with a different form of prayer which would owe more to the parish or so-called 'cathedral' form.

Communal and ecclesial

The rather feeble aspiration of SC 100 that the Prayer of the Church become a more regular feature of parish life was never realistically considered during the reform.[22] Despite regulating for private recitation, GILH 20 clearly stated that the 'Liturgy of the Hours, like the other liturgical services, is not a private function'. A small but growing number of parish and other communities are beginning to find in the Hours a valuable form of common prayer. Religious in community will always need to engage in regular prayer together, but this can be celebrated in a parish community that is served by a community or as part of the Daily Prayer that is prayed with lay collaborators in ministry. By using a cathedral or popular form of the Liturgy of the Hours (especially in pastoral contexts), work, ministry, and community are bound together in such a way that these too can grow to be extensions of praise while being nourished in ecclesial prayer.

Individual religious, caught up with busy pastoral ministry, cannot always be present with the community of which they are a member when it prays. However, in the Pauline sense, they and the community from which they are unavoidably absent both exercise the same priesthood of Christ, with Christ. They are both, in two different ways, involved in the same 'priestly and missionary service' of God: one through pastoral ministry in the

---

[21] See Taft, *The Liturgy of the Hours in East and West*, p. 364. For a spirituality of praying the Hours, see Paul Bradshaw, *Two Ways of Praying: Introducing Liturgical Spirituality* (London: SPCK, 1995).

[22] *SC* 100 needs to be read also in the context of *SC* 27: 'It must be emphasized that rites which are meant to be celebrated in common, with the faithful present and actively participating, should as far as possible be celebrated in that way rather than by an individual and quasi-privately.'

service of God's mission which takes them from their habitual liturgical assembly; the other through a liturgical participation in this same mission. Fidelity to the Hours, even for those who are canonically bound to them, must be seen primarily in its ecclesial and quasi-sacramental sense, rather in terms of fulfilment of law.

The ecclesial nature of the Prayer of the Church is not based on regulation or any random consideration. All liturgies, by their very nature, 'are not private functions but are celebrations of the church' (SC 26). The challenge here is for regular assemblies to move beyond 'praying in common' to a place where they will begin to engage in 'common prayer'.

Many religious, at least in this part of the world, tend to be reticent about engaging ritually with liturgy, in the wrong belief that ritual is artificial or of secondary importance. Ritual is, in fact, the principal mode of communication we employ when relating to one another in normal daily human intercourse. In the absence of a ritual element, Daily Prayer has become for many a mere cerebral affair, and confined to the recitation of prayer texts. The traditional cathedral forms would have used light, procession, incense, sign of peace, bodily attitudes (such as bowing for doxology, and kneeling for penitential psalms outside of Easter season), singing, and a diversity of appropriate ministry. Some of these elements can be adopted in ways that facilitate the liturgical prayer of communities.

Learning to praise

As Roman Catholics, we need to learn how to celebrate liturgy for its own sake, without expecting something back in return, and with the sole purpose of offering praise and thanksgiving to God. The Second Vatican Council, by speaking of liturgy and sacraments in the context of salvation history and participation in the paschal mystery of Christ, corrected the medieval view which was predominant in theology. This stated that, whereas 'sacraments' were occasions for receiving grace from God, liturgy was that movement of ourselves towards God, offering him the adoration and worship required as a duty of religion. In contrast, the Liturgy Constitution presents all liturgy (which includes sacraments) to be a participation in Christ's salvific mystery as part of our response to God's prior invitation in Christ. The Council also refrained from defining liturgy in juridical terms.

This 'sacrifice of praise' (Psalms 140/141:2) is embodied in our lifestyle and our ministries (see Romans 12:1), all of which, in turn, can become embodiments of praise that flow from and back into our praying of the Hours. The liturgy is not the only place of encounter with the paschal mystery, but it is the privileged arena wherein we transact salvifically with the world and the society of which we are part.

The Prayer of the Church creates a context for meaning

As members of Christ, religious share with the baptised in Christ's mission to establish the reign of God, achieved definitively in Christ, but in these last times, the *eschaton*, needing to take root in the lives of everybody, in every generation, culture and social environment. The efficacy of the paschal mystery of Christ guarantees the transformation of all of creation and serves 'for the life of the world'. The project that we call 'religious life' is lodged at the heart of this salvific dynamic, and it is here that we find our metanarrative.

Psalms constitute a central component of the Liturgy of the Hours. The narrative that these psalms and the scripture readings provide forms us more deeply in the ecclesial sense of what the reign is about. Related to this is the realisation that narrative, as we read it today, is never the pure unadulterated communication of a past event. Our retelling, through scriptures and the psalms, of the metanarrative of the paschal mystery can take on a type of faith-autobiography of the 'pray-er', and are 'read' in terms of the social, political, cultural, and economic contexts in which we find ourselves today. The psalms are not necessarily about 'spirituality', or about heaven or 'other-worldly' realities. They are extremely 'human' expressions which articulate a whole range of human emotions and feelings, occasionally not even leaving God 'off the hook' but demanding of God an account for past deeds done. In a unique way, the psalms allow for some level of affective prayer in the context of the more formal ecclesial liturgy.[23]

By exercising our baptismal priesthood in offering praise and thanksgiving to God for its own sake, by placing before God the needs of the world in which 'we live, and move and have our Christian being', we engage with the perennial *hodie* (today-ness) aspect of our religious life, caught up as it is in its entanglement with the salvific mystery of Christ through which we are propelled into our future in God, now.

CONCLUSION

We do not celebrate liturgy simply for its own sake. Liturgy is nothing more than encountering the living God in Christ. The Spirit of the Risen Lord transforms 'this gathering' of people into this *ecclesial assembly called by the mystery of Christ to participate in the mission of God*. The liturgical assembly is where we meet with 'world', and 'world' is how we live paschal mystery: it is where we incarnate, through the Spirit, the Body of Christ; it is how we engage with salvation. The purpose of this 'coming together' as church is not simply to add a religious dimension to individual lives, but rather to embody Christ's vision of the world redeemed. The mandate to 'pray without ceasing' is addressed also to religious who have traditionally given public and ecclesial expression to this through their celebration of the Prayer of the Church.

Religious are called to pray daily as church 'for the life of the world'.

---

[23] See Murphy, 'Reading/Reciting the Psalms', pp. 638–9.

Reflection Questions

1. 'The liturgical life of the church is integral to the "mission of God" in which the church (including professed religious) is obliged to participate by virtue of baptism.' What do you understand by this? What bearing does it have on your participation in the Prayer of the Church?

2. What do you understand by 'Western liturgical privatisation and Eucharistic excess'? Why does the author suggest that this is a problem?

3. What does the author say about religious reciting the Prayer of the Church? What has been your experience of this? How has it impacted on religious life for you?

8

Epilogue I

Vatican II – Whose Inheritance?

Gemma Simmonds CJ

Epilogue II, which follows these editorial remarks, was not a paper originally offered at the Heythrop Symposium at which all the rest of the papers featured in this book were discussed. It is an abridged version of an essay written by a Trappist monk, Dom Erik Varden, now acting abbot of the Cistercian monastery of Mount Saint Bernard in Leicestershire, who was present as a symposium participant. It seems to me important, in a collection of reflections on the fiftieth anniversary of the Second Vatican Council, to hear the voice of a religious who was not born when it began. The essay is a prolonged reflection on the dynamic of continuity and change, beginning with an overview of Pope John Paul II's apostolic letter *Orientale Lumen* of 1995 in which he speaks of the urgent need for East–West dialogue. Varden uses this as an analogy for the need of different sorts of dialogue within religious communities, a dialogue that can potentially transcend tensions presented by differing ecclesiologies.

One matter which emerges repeatedly during the rest of the chapters in this book is that of dialogue, or the lack of it, between groups within the church representing the 'hermeneutic of discontinuity' (or rupture) and the 'hermeneutic of continuity'. These are otherwise known, most unhelpfully, as 'liberals' and 'conservatives' or 'reformers' and 'restorationists' or whatever label each side prefers to give the other. This means those who, on the whole, see the Second Vatican Council as the best thing to happen to the church since its foundation, and those who view it, or at least its subsequent interpretation, with a more critical air,

149

as the source of many of the church's current troubles. In the revision stage of the symposium papers Varden offered a critique of a certain looseness in the use of the word 'church' as an unidentified 'them' opposed in various ways to an equally unclear 'us', which he had picked up from participants during discussions. Many present, both on that day and the public study day which followed, were painfully aware of the recent tensions between the Congregation for the Doctrine of the Faith and women religious in the United States of America. The majority of them were women religious, some speaking from the perspective of the frequent difficulty they themselves encounter in having their voice and experience taken seriously within the church.

Archbishop Tobin was both honest and measured in his even-handed response to concerns raised, and the news of his departure from the Vatican dicastery for consecrated life was greeted with much regret by those present. In his own chapter in the book he distinguishes between what many call 'the institutional church', and 'the church where we hear the Word of God and celebrate the sacraments of life', referring also to the presence within the faith community of 'some values ... that lead the Lord today to look at us and say, "But it can't be that way among you."' He goes on to exhort religious to model a different sort of church.

Many of my generation and that above mine joined or stayed within religious life precisely because it offered them a space within the believing community where they could do just that. There is evidence that suggests that religious life, by its very origin, began as a flight not only from the world but from a church that had allied itself with the power structures of the Empire and all that it represented. This is disputed by some modern patristic scholars who point to the symbiotic relationship that grew up early between Empire and monastery, but it is perhaps not surprising that we still find a certain tension between what sees itself as central and what sees itself as liminal within the church.

The modelling of a 'different church' has also been a constant theme of Pope Francis, the first member of a religious order to become Pope in over one hundred years. He is clearly not afraid to take unilateral decisions when he feels it necessary, but he also appears able to act on his direct experience of a more consultative model of governance. Pope Francis has regularly called upon leaders in the church, religious and clergy alike, to leave the safety of presbytery and convent and go out into the streets to learn the wisdom of those to whom they are missioned. His preference for a 'bruised, hurting and dirty' church has breathed fresh air into many corners of the church, while also resonating strongly with the founding charisms of many religious congregations.[1]

The Vatican Council's Decree on the Eastern Catholic Churches, *Orientalium Ecclesiarum*, reminds us that 'variety within the Church not only does no harm to its unity, but rather makes it manifest'.[2] While this was originally meant in quite another context, it would be well for us to remember it amid the increasingly polarised stances within the community of the faithful, many of them based on culturally coded articulations of both belief and practice. Erik Varden, far shorter in the religious tooth than most present, points out that 'the mystery of the church, insofar as it continuously manifests the grace of the incarnation, transcends any particularism of culture'. This is, of course, true, but religious life has never been lived in a culturally neutral vacuum. The inability or unwillingness of cultures within religious life to meet one another half or even quarter of the way is a danger to which many current commentators are pointing and is, in my own opinion, a grave threat to its survival.

Archbishop Tobin points to this in the case he cites of older religious disparaging many of those seeking their vocation today as 'right wing nuts'. Like many of my generation and those older than me, passionate about the Council that promised renewal and liberation from suffocating modes of living, believing and praying, it can be deeply painful to encounter what feels like the dismissive judgementalism of some who clamour for 'traditions' that are nothing of the sort. When we encounter such attitudes from the central authority within the church it becomes easy to blame something called 'the institutional church' without being

---

[1] Pope Francis, *Evangelii Gaudium*, 49.

[2] Pope Paul VI, *Orientalium Ecclesiarum*, 2.

too nuanced about who or what we are referring to. During a recent BBC broadcast discussing the apostolic visitation of the women religious of America I was asked why, if I and other religious like me objected to it so much, we didn't leave the church. I found myself replying, 'Because we are the church.' However disenfranchised some Vatican II warriors may at times feel, this is the problem.

Orientale Lumen reminds us that among us dialogue is not an option but an obligation. That cuts both ways. Acts like the recent doctrinal assessment of the Leadership Conference of Women Religious or the imposition of the new liturgy, with its regrettably revisionist overtones, with little or no consultation of bishops, let alone laity, are a cause of painful and genuine alienation to many faithful religious. For them, as for many of the laity, the discrepancy between the perceived ferocity of discipline against religious like Jeannine Grammick or Leonardo Boff contrasts shockingly with the years of impunity enjoyed by clerical child abusers. The effective ignoring of Sr Maura O'Donohue MMM's memo 'Urgent Concerns for the Church in the Context of HIV/AIDS' also troubled many seasoned members of missionary orders who had witnessed similar situations to those outlined in the memo.[3] Official intervention in such urgent cases as the memo records was thought inadvisable, while direct curial intervention in the governance of religious orders whose members were seen as 'out of line' became more common. This also contrasted with the apparently uncritical favour bestowed from Rome on new 'ecclesial movements', many of which have been characterised by a spirit very different from that of the Second Vatican Council.

But if that is a profile of the problem from one end of the spectrum, there is also another perspective. New religious entering religious orders today and seeking the Prayer of the Church or regular sacramental practice in community may be

---

[3] Sr Maura O'Donohue MMM, 'Urgent Concerns for the Church in the Context of HIV/AIDS', *National Catholic Reporter Online* [website], 9 March 2001
<http://natcath.org/NCR_Online/documents/UrgentConcernsO'DO NOHUE.htm>

told that community liturgies should be based on self-expression, and find themselves in the middle of a dance to the sun instead of at Lauds. Any question of reclaiming religious dress is dismissed as religious mania or sexual repression, while the desire to live in community is seen as infantile institutionalism and codependency. These are caricatures, of course, but there is enough truth in them to point to the painful reality of a cultural dialogue of the deaf.

In the epilogue that follows the reader is invited to listen with open mind and heart to this reflection on dialogue. The encyclical on which the first half of its original version is based uncompromisingly censors the scandal of division among Christians while there rises from all parts of the globe to heaven the bewildered cry of men and women seeking truth. The churches have an obligation to answer with a single voice, pointing unequivocally to Christ. If we perpetuate motives of strife that weaken our credibility we fail to help those faith-seekers who long to find the way to God. The present moment calls for concrete gestures rather than words, through which the men and women of our times might be healed, reconciled and unified.

Orientale Lumen urges us to respond to the needs of today's humanity by becoming men and women of communion. Erik Varden observes that this challenge is explicitly addressed to religious and especially concerns monks as 'essentially [men of] communion'. The monastery, he says, has a call to be a 'prophetic place in which creation becomes praise of God, in which the law of charity, lived out in practice, becomes an ideal of human fellowship'. A community of monks has the potential to be 'a wonderful bridge of fraternity'. Out of the living experience of communion, Christians may expect something entirely new to arise, even at the level of institutions. Restored unity between the churches, we are told, may take a form unlike anything the world has known. As the Body of Christ recovers its integrity, it will learn to breathe differently.

On the basis of the image of 'breathing differently', Varden turns to consider the millennial history of his own order. Through the figures of Saints Stephen Harding and Bernard of Clairvaux and their contrasting approaches to this history, he demonstrates that innovation and tradition feed, and do not devour, one another. They are engaged in ongoing, life-giving conversation. This model may equally well stand for a dialogue of different generational cultures within the church as we experience it. This is the voice of a generation for whom, historically, Vatican II is as distant as the Syllabus of Errors was to those of us who enthusiastically embraced the Council. If we advocate and commit ourselves to a 'church of dialogue' then listening to that voice and trying to understand the theological and spiritual values that lie behind it must also be part of our commitment.

9

Epilogue II

The Challenge of History

Erik Varden OCSO

Then

Communion presupposes remembrance. Not only must I embrace the other in the fullness of his present truth; I must understand what has made him; and I must know what has made me. The quest for self-knowledge is deeply rooted in the legacy of Cîteaux. We know it as a theme in St Bernard's treatise on the Steps of Humility and Pride. The imperative formulated by this text, however, had informed the Cistercian project since its inception. According to the *Exordium Parvum*, a key factor motivating Robert, Alberic, Stephen and the rest while still at Molesmes was a crisis of identity, a sense of being trapped in contradiction. Having pledged to observe the Benedictine Rule in all particulars, they were prisoners of circumstances that rendered such observance impossible. Not only did they desire a stricter way of life; they felt bound to it. The alternative, they thought, was to live as perjurers (III). At the same time, they recognised that other ways were legitimate for other men. The willingness of Robert to resume the abbacy at Molesmes is proof good enough. When Pope Urban II asked him to return, it was by way of request, not of command. Robert heeded the pontiff's wish, but would hardly have done so had he really thought he forfeited his salvation. As for the brethren who followed him, they went along simply because they 'did not like' the new monastery (VII). From that moment, healthy discernment marked the spirit of Cîteaux. The founders' aim was fidelity to an ancient code of practice. Would this oblige them to reject anything not explicitly warranted by it? What is it to be faithful? What is it to be authentic? By pursuing these questions (if only a short way), we shall learn something about the status of tradition at early Cîteaux.

On the face of it, the Cistercian project was conservative in scope, retrospective in motivation. Yet its protagonists made ground-breaking innovations. We may recognise two main trends within this process. The first trend consisted in a systematic appeal to established authorities. Of these, the most obvious was the Rule of St Benedict. The *Exordium Parvum* provides a succinct account of the manner in which the community approached it. It gives the impression of seamen setting sail on a crisp, clear day, joyfully throwing overboard any ballast threatening to hamper speedy progress. The emphasis is not on grim-faced 'strict observance' but on the shedding of encumbrances. Furs, fine frocks and feather beds: let the current take them! Benefices and privileges went the same way (XV). Robert and his companions had passed through the stage of forming a resolve. They knew they did not need staff, purse or two tunics, and so were happy to do without. We may be best placed to appreciate the *puritas regulae* to which they aspired if we understand 'pure' not in cultic, but in ecological terms. Our founders did not so much undertake to 'purify' what had been 'profaned' – that point of view came in later. They sought to taste the sweetness of an alpine wellspring whose waters, further down, had lost its savour through the presence in the watercourse of dead wood and picnic remains – things neutral in themselves but corrupting when left to decay. These men breathed the air of the summit. Their requirements were unlike those of the dwellers on the plain. It has been well said that the original project of Cîteaux was not of reform but of innovation. We sense as much in the founders' fondness for calling their house 'the New Monastery'. They were not, at this stage, primarily reacting against anything or anyone. Poor followers of the poor Christ, they followed their master towards heights hitherto unseen.

This thirst for the savour of origins likewise characterised the two great research projects which, under Abbot Stephen, the monks of Cîteaux initiated in the interest of *puritas*: the revision of the Latin Scriptures and the first Cistercian chant reform. Both undertakings were remarkable. That this small, provincial community should harbour a wish to possess better editions of the Bible and liturgical books seems audacious enough. That they took matters into their own hands is staggering. Without even having finished the monastery, Abbot Stephen invested precious resources in a complicated, time-consuming mission that involved lengthy absences for several brethren as they travelled to Milan, Metz, and elsewhere searching for manuscripts. His decision tells us much about the community's priorities. They deemed it indispensable to lay their foundations on the *auctoritas* of tradition. Stephen's method was thorough and scholarly. He collated the best manuscripts he could find, then compared and contrasted them to establish 'authorised' versions for public use. Sometimes findings were perplexing. Reliable sources contained readings at odds with contemporary expectations of coherence. In such cases, Stephen and his collaborators trusted authority rather than their judgement. They did not, however, stand back from fresh thinking. On the contrary, the safeguarding of tradition required innovation. To ensure material self-sufficiency without detriment to regular observance, the first Cistercians adopted and developed the institution of 'bearded laybrothers', unthought of by St Benedict. They thereby helped change the shape of Western monasticism.

Another relative novelty embraced by Cîteaux and her daughters was the idea of a general chapter with structures of responsibility and answerability. We may extend our simile: once our founders had cleared the debris that muddied the water from the spring, they freely redirected its flow for maximum benefit. Their attitude to tradition was at once responsible and free. They engaged with it in dialogue. The attitude I have outlined (the 'ecological' reading of *puritas regulae*) is closely linked to the figure of St Stephen Harding. He was a man of rich experience who had lived as a monk in several houses; he possessed solid, varied learning; he had known what it was to grow lukewarm and to rekindle the flame of commitment. He stands before us as well-rounded and whole, 'courteous in speech, of joyful countenance, his heart ever rejoicing in the Lord'. With the second generation of Cistercians, something changes. A new trend makes its presence felt, an understanding of monastic *puritas* that increasingly demands segregation of the pure from the impure, of wheat from chaff, sheep from goats. Its chief proponent was St Bernard, who, unlike Stephen, seems never to have known wavering. He appeared as a kind of saviour from the moment he entered Cîteaux, and spent only some twenty months in the habit without being an abbot. For all his dislike of scholastic methods, Bernard had much in common with the tendency of the schools. His confidence in principles affected his understanding of monastic and ecclesial life. Of necessity, it also informed his response to tradition.

We find a salient example of this in the second Cistercian chant reform, instigated in the early 1140s. Although not a trained musician, the abbot of Clairvaux was asked to oversee the work, whose rationale he explained in a letter: the musical scores that resulted from St Stephen's work appeared corrupt since many melodies diverged from the laws of modality. Their mixed modal character made them into monstrous hybrids, unfit for cultic service. Thus new versions were called for. Significant remarks! Bernard and his committee had an a priori idea of what constituted correct chant. When the manuscripts did not correspond to these ideas, they rejected the *auctoritas* rather than their principles. They sought a single 'authentic' source. When research revealed, rather, considerable variety, they thought the whole corpus corrupt and reconstituted it from scratch. The procedure is evidently problematic. The plainchant then in liturgical use largely antedated the mid-ninth century, when musical scholars began to elaborate the ideas on which Bernard relied and which twentieth-century scholarship has shown to be flawed. Yet on this basis the reformers assembled the *Regule de arte musica* by which the repertoire was 'amended', sometimes disastrously. I am not trying to idealise the first reform. It was executed in a hurry, largely by non-specialists. The sources on which it was based were not the best. My point does not concern the relative outcome of the two reforms but the principles on which they were based. In the first, critical judgement bowed to *auctoritas*; in the second, *auctoritas* was subject to critical judgement.

This priority of principle accounts for much in Bernard's achievement that is puzzling, not least what Peter Dinzelbacher, whose Germanic scholarship is not given to frivolity, calls his 'intense urge to interfere'. Here is a man who fervently upheld the need for monks to submit to their local ordinary, yet spent much of his career arranging episcopal appointments to suit himself; who was jealous of abbatial authority, yet spontaneously usurped that of his own father immediate, the Abbot of Cîteaux, as in the famous incident of 1124 when Abbot Arnold of Morimond left his abbey for the Holy Land; who, when the monk Drogo left his Benedictine house of profession at Reims for Pontigny, wrote to the affected abbot deploring such behaviour (Ep. 32.1) while at the same time congratulating Drogo on his 'perfection' (Ep. 34.1). 'Nothing', said Bernard, 'that concerns God lies beyond the scope of my attention' (Ep. 20). His trust in his own judgement could make him very flexible in the observance of conventional procedures he otherwise professed to uphold. His understanding of the church's needs drove him increasingly to adopt inflexible positions that involved acrimonious controversy. His sense of 'purity' led him readily to condemn his opponents, be they monks, ecclesiastics or secular rulers, as 'impure'. It led him to absolutise the Cistercian ideal as he saw it. What had started out as one path among many seemed to him increasingly the only path.

Now

Our brief examination of these two perspectives on tradition – the enquiring and the polemic, that of Stephen and that of Bernard – does not imply a judgement. The two complement one another, sometimes in creative tension, sometimes in conflict: the relationship between Stephen and Bernard was, after all, ambivalent. We see both tendencies recurring at key moments in our order's history. The question imposes itself: what about us? We stand, I believe, at a crossroads, with a choice to make. I shall sketch the contours of that choice by indicating three aspects of Cistercian life in the contemporary church as I experience it. The qualifier is important. I am not presenting an objective analysis, merely my contribution to a conversation in which we all take part. As such it will take us back to our first theme, on the gift and challenge of communion.

The first point is this: when I entered the monastery, I was keenly aware of entering a history of rupture. It was communicated to me anecdotally on a daily basis. Most aspects of observance and liturgical practice invited comparison with 'the old days', which for some, so I understood, represented a primitive stage in monastic evolution where the law had not yet been tempered by grace, others spoke of it as a lost Eden barred by fiery swords. Whatever the emotional charge of 'now' and 'then', the gap was palpably there. The decree of unification had altered the canonical structure of the community; the redefinition of silence alongside the abandonment of dormitories and scriptoria had affected the nature of fraternal relations; the liturgy had been invented from zero; evolving positions in theology had reformulated the very nature of Cistercian life. People had come and gone, and not only in the novitiate and juniorate. From 1950 to today, our community has seen fifty-nine solemn professions and two transfers. In the same period, twenty-nine brethren in solemn vows have left monastic life. Even the topography of the house was eloquent. Hardly a single room functions today as it did fifty years ago. For a novice, the sea change seemed bewildering. Amid such upheaval, which are the lines of continuity that really matter?

The second point concerns the generation gap in our monasteries. It affects us as it affects communities throughout the Western church. It is not a phenomenon unique to the present. We have known it before, both globally and in our own house. Yet the present gap is especially significant for the extraordinary events that occurred, as it were, in the middle of it. I think of a recent statement by Dom Simon McGurk:

> In 1962 came the greatest event in the history of the world since the Council of Jerusalem, the Second Vatican Council. Now, 41 years after the end of the Council, no one who was not around

then could understand the sheer power of the Spirit rushing through the churches. It was definitely good for us to be there. The speed with which the Spirit moved the hearts of those great bishops emerging from obscurity, the theologians, the liturgists and ecumenists, was like a cruise missile. It was indeed frightening to some but was new life to most. Now, instead of the Divine Office being prayed by rote, it came alive; the Mass became 'ours'.[1]

My response to this rhetoric is mixed. The dismissal of nineteen centuries of Christian experience is evidently absurd. It is untrue to imply that no progress was made in theology, liturgy and ecumenism before 1962. Yet what to me is most objectionable is the 'hermetic' reading of the Council itself. The spiritual impact of Vatican II is reified, made into a fundamentally unsharable possession. McGurk's final sentence is revealing. 'The Mass became ours,' he says, as if the mere fact of 'being around' in the sixties conferred proprietorship. The flimsiest awareness of church history exposes all this as nonsense. And yet, on a superficial level, is there some truth in what is said? For those of us untimely born, the Council is experientially inaccessible as a watershed. We have no choice but to see it as one manifestation of the Spirit among many. It is interesting that this 'hermeneutic of continuity' is now championed by the highest authority.

My third point arises out of the other two and concerns post-conciliar inculturation. The term has recently been much in vogue and is rightly understood as an unqualified good. But has not the post-conciliar experience of the Western church revealed a potential pitfall on the way? McGurk's 'cruise missile' left an open hole waiting to be filled. The sheer magnitude of possibility, novelty and freedom must have been intoxicating. It has resulted, however, in established forms of Catholic life, prayer, song, and ritual that, more than in any previous age, are peculiarly locked in time, and an unusual time at that. The late sixties and early seventies brought transformation to Europe and America, a movement inspiring fast reaction and counter-reaction. Literary,

---

[1] *Touched by God: Ten Monastic Journeys*, Laurentia Johns, ed., (London: Burns and Oates, 2008), p. 169 f.

aesthetic, spiritual and social ideals were 'in' one day, 'out' the next. How could this climate not affect the church, which had opened all doors and windows to let air in? Many texts, tunes, fireworks-patterned carpets and community manifestos that must have seemed fresh and 'relevant' in the aftermath of 1965 today appear touchingly antiquated, monuments to the ephemeral. This fact reveals the fragility of in-sub-culturation. It teaches us that Christian engagement with culture must touch the still waters of the depths, not the froth washed up on beaches.

The situation I have described was recently presented to us visually when a visitor to Gethsemani showed us a series of slides from that great monastery. As the Order's flagship in the US, Gethsemani, Merton's 'heart of America', must be the most photographed abbey in the world. Books, cards and leaflets produced there in the forties and fifties present beautiful icons of monasticism: careful compositions of mock-medieval interiors filled with cowled giants performing dramatic gestures. It is not difficult to see what exercised a romantic attraction on Merton and many others. There is not much romance in the appearance of Gethsemani today. Stark, square formations of steel, brick and concrete-embedded gravel have replaced the *hommage* to idealised monastic timelessness. Instead of ethereal hooded shades we see efficient-looking blokes in overalls making fruitcakes. Even the pigeon by the pond is of cast metal. This projection, too, is eloquent. It speaks of monks as ordinary, business-minded people who have a job to do and get on with it. But is Gethsemani II more 'Cistercian' than Gethsemani I? I think not. Both represent interpretations of our heritage based on the tastes, moods and expectations of their times. Gethsemani II owes, I submit, no more to the spirit of primitive Cîteaux than to the sensibility and functional ethos that produced Milton Keynes, the Barbican, and the Coalville Arcade. It presents, in the sense defined above, a polemic reading of Cistercian life. Further, it only really works as a statement when compared with the old. It is the memory of the former, Gothic interior that makes its replacement seem 'purified' or 'reformed'. To one who enters it fresh, it appears simply as a rather forbidding empty space.

The same could be said, *mutatis mutandis*, about much post-conciliar 'deconstruction'. Every week the Catholic press writes (The *Herald* with glee, *The Tablet* with alarm) about current efforts to recapture 'tradition', especially on the part of Catholics born after 1965. What does this tell us? It tells us, I think, that some issues that were contentious forty years ago are not issues any more. They should be laid to rest. It tells us that each generation has the need to appropriate tradition on its own terms, based on its own needs. It tells us that the post-conciliar experience of radical change is being refined by an appeal to continuity. It tells us that many of the faithful want the church not only to dialogue with society but to offer it direction, drawing on centuries of experience to give purpose, colour and beauty to our times. It tells us, above all, that the church's tradition is a living thing, exceeding the grasp of any group, any generation. The moment I think I possess tradition, that it depends on me, it dies. What joy that nine hundred years of Cistercian experience equip us to live the present challenge full of hope! From corporate experience, we know of the life-giving ebb and flow of innovation and tradition. After a period of Bernardine redefinition based on first principles, the example of Stephen's intelligent assimilation of history may be prophetic to our times. By persevering in his school, we may hope to tap into the radicalism, joy and energy of 'the New Monastery', singing a new song to Christ, the bright dawn of a new creation.